THE CONFESSIONS
OF A DANCING GIRL

THE CONFESSIONS
OF A DANCING GIRL

BY HERSELF

HEATH, CRANTON & OUSELEY, LTD
FLEET LANE · LONDON · E.C.

CONTENTS

Chaper   *Page*

    I. I Run Away 7
   II. Apprenticed to an Acrobat . 29
  III. Life in the Profession . . . 48
  IV. How I became a Dancer . . 67
    V. My Spanish Admirer . . . 87
  VI. Adventures in Spain . . . 108
 VII. The Student of Coimbra . 126
VIII. My Portuguese Hosts . . . 147
  IX. Hard Times in London . . . 157
   X. With a Troupe in America . 177

THE CONFESSIONS OF A DANCING GIRL

CHAPTER I

I RUN AWAY

I WAS born in 1887 in Camden Town. My parents had three children, all girls, and I was the eldest. I cannot remember my mother well, for she died when I was quite a child; but I have been told that she was a good woman, and greatly devoted to her children. I do not wish to speak or think harshly of my father. He may be still alive; but I have not seen him since I began my career in the circus and on the stage. He kept a public-house at the time when I was born. The business failed, and he lost money and left us in great poverty soon after the death of my mother. In a short time my father married again, and I saw nothing of him for several months.

I suppose I was about four years old when I was sent to my mother's stepmother. I can remember her faintly, and my recollections of her are that she treated me kindly. For three or four years I was sent from one relative to another.

One of them I can recall more clearly—a hard, scolding woman who beat me severely for the slightest fault. I have a remembrance of my unhappiness throughout all those childhood days; and, with the exception of my mother's stepmother, I cannot recall to mind any woman who ever "mothered" me, or showed any tenderness or love. I do not think that I was a very naughty, difficult child, though no doubt I caused my different guardians some worry and trouble. Whippings and cuffings were more common in those days than loving words and caresses. Nobody wanted me, and most of my relations found trouble in making both ends meet.

I am very fond of children, and when I think that there are hundreds, perhaps thousands, of little boys and girls living the sort of life that I passed through up to the age of twelve, it makes me sad. God help the unprotected, motherless child in this hard world!

I have never understood why my father appeared suddenly, after a long absence, and took me away from my aunt, who was looking after me. Had he repented for the neglect of his children?

I recall his coming late one night, and stealing me from bed, and carrying me off to the woman whom he had married. My life with my stepmother was not very unhappy; she was not unkind at first. But when she had children of her own, I think she regarded me as an interloper and a nuisance, and no doubt she was poor, and unable to provide for me as well as her own children.

It was at this time that I was sent to school. My parents were Roman Catholics, and I attended a convent school in London as a day scholar. My education was meagre; I just learned to spell, read and write, and that is all the schooling I ever had. All that I know I have learned from the many men and women I have met in my travels in this country and abroad, and from the books that I have read. But very few books came into my hands when I was young.

One day my father again disappeared mysteriously. I cannot say whether he afterwards returned to his second wife. This was the beginning of a new series of changes for me, and I went to live with my grandfather, who was married for the third time. This home was no better than the others, for I was often cruelly beaten and ill-treated.

I suppose I was a spirited child; at any rate, life became so unbearable that I made up my mind to run away. Quite distinctly, I remember slipping out of the house in the fog of a winter afternoon, and wandering through long, dreary streets in the North of London. I had no plans, and no idea where I was going to spend the night. I had escaped from my grandfather and his wife, and that was all that I cared about. But after wandering for hours, I began to feel hungry. How well I have known that feeling of hunger at different times of my life! The hunger grew worse and worse, and I was getting very tired.

Presently I sat down on a doorstep in a quiet street. I cannot remember the name of the street, but it was a long way from where I lived. People passed me and took no notice. I was only a little, ill-dressed girl. It was quite dark now, and I began to feel lonely. Perhaps I sobbed; I think it is most likely that my loneliness and hunger made me cry. At last, a passing policeman stopped and turned the light of his bull's-eye on me as I crouched on the cold stones.

"What's the matter?" he asked in a gruff though kindly voice.

"Please, I am so hungry!" was my reply.

"What's your name?" he asked.

"Marion," I answered.

He tried to find out where I lived, but I would not tell him, for I did not mean to return to my grandfather's tenement.

"You had better come with me," the constable said.

Taking my chilled little hand in his, he

led me to the nearest police-station, where I was received by the inspector and other officers, and perched on a chair by the fire. After some discussion, to which I listened intently, I heard the words:

"Better take her to the workhouse."

This frightened me very much, for I had a fancy that when once you enter a workhouse there is no coming out.

"Oh, please don't take me there!" I begged, with tears.

But I was led through several streets, sobbing, till we reached a great building with hundreds of gaslit windows. And presently I was in charge of the matron, who tried to comfort me, and gave me into the care of a woman, who undressed me and put me to bed in a ward full of other little friendless children.

My stay in the workhouse was short. About noon the next day my grandmother who had been making inquiries at the police-station, came to take me home. She described me to the wardress as a naughty, unmanageable child, and as soon as we were in the street she began to threaten me with fearful punishment for running away.

"I'll give you something when I get you home!" was her repeated threat.

She took me, trembling and white, into the house.

"Look at her!" she cried to my grandfather. "There's a child for you! Run away, will you?" And as she spoke she struck me in the face, knocking me on to the floor.

All that night I lay sobbing in bed.

The harshness with which my grandmother treated me was perhaps the cause of my going on the stage. If I had been brought up by my mother, who was a loving, kind-hearted woman, my life would, no doubt, have been a very different one; and it is possible that I should have been put to a trade, such as millinery or dressmaking. I cannot remember that I had any strong hankering as a child for a stage career. But at the age of twelve, after a most unhappy childhood, I realized that nobody really wanted me. I was considered an encumbrance and a nuisance.

My relations were all poor, and I was just another mouth that had to be filled. It is a common story; but there are people who do not know how the poor orphaned children, born of poor parents, suffer in body and mind.

I well remember the day when I slipped out of my grandmother's house, filled with a determination to escape for ever. There seemed to me no occupation so easy and attractive as the music-hall stage. Once or twice I had been taken by friends to a music-hall, where I had seen some of the leading comic singers, wonderful acrobats, and nimble dancers. But it was that day for the first time that I thought of the stage as a profession. I had to earn a living somehow. How could a child expect to get work? I knew no trade, and I was really too young to obtain a situation of any sort.

"There is nothing but the stage," I said to myself, as I walked quickly through the streets of North London. I cannot remember how I came into the possession of twopence, but I know that this was the amount of my fortune on that day. With this twopence I bought a copy of the *Stage*.

Entering a quiet churchyard, where there were seats under the trees, I sat down and turned over the pages of the paper until I found the advertisement columns. How often I have searched those columns since that day twelve years ago! And how much I have learned, seen, and done since that morning.

There were plenty of advertisements for actresses, singers, and chorus girls; but I knew that I was too young to act, and, of course, I had no knowledge of music. My only chance seemed to lie in the circus profession or on the variety stage.

After bending for a long time over the paper, I found this notice: "Wanted immediately, girl of ten or twelve as apprentice to acrobatics. Apply Mademoiselle Elvierra."

The address was somewhere in Balham. I have quite forgotten the name of the street. I jumped up in a great state of excitement. I was only just twelve years of age, and I looked even younger. I imagine myself as a thin, ill-fed child, and I am sure that I was badly dressed.

" Where is Balham ? How can I get there ? " was my thought as I hurried from the churchyard.

I inquired the way from the first kind-looking woman whom I met. She looked a little surprised.

" It's a long way," she said. " You'd better take a bus."

" I've no money," I said.

She directed me as well as she was able, and I started off, walking over Blackfriars Bridge. By repeatedly inquiring the way, I reached Balham in the afternoon, and found the road in which Mademoiselle Elvierra lodged. It was a dingy street, and the lodgings were third-rate and frowsy. The woman who admitted me said: " Are you an acrobat ? "

" I want to be one," I answered.

" Go in there," she said, pointing to a door.

I went into the room, and saw a woman with very yellow hair, untidily dressed, who was talking to a girl of about my own age.

"No, it's no use," said mademoiselle firmly; "I can't take you without your parents' consent. You'd better go home."

The child's eyes filled with tears as she turned from the room. Without speaking, she went out. A great fear came over me, for how was I to obtain my parents' consent? My mother was dead, and I knew nothing of the whereabouts of my father. I felt that I was shaking with nervousness as Mademoiselle Elvierra's eyes looked into mine. What could I say? I had not thought of this hindrance to my entering the artiste's life.

"Well, who are you?" asked the acrobat, eyeing me very closely.

I told her my name, and that I wanted to go on the stage.

Possibly she was struck with my build, or she may have thought that I was intelligent and likely to become a good pupil.

"What about your mother?" she inquired.

"Oh, she doesn't mind," I gasped out.

"You'd have to come for five years at least."

"I wouldn't mind that."

"Well, get your mother to come and see me. I think you and I would get on well together, my dear."

A sudden flash of hope had come into my mind. I remembered that I had a married cousin at Chelsea, who had two children. She was a very kind woman. I resolved upon a desperate plan. I would see this cousin, and get her to impersonate my mother, and to consent to my becoming Mademoiselle Elvierra's apprentice.

"When will you bring your mother?" she asked. "I'm starting for Liverpool on Sunday for a week's work, and I want this thing fixed up at once. Do you understand?"

"Yes," I said eagerly. "I'll bring my mother along quickly—as soon as I can."

The woman patted my cheek, and called me a good girl. She was rather a good-looking woman, and the fact that she was a performer almost overawed me. I smiled up at her shyly, and then hurried away to the back street in Chelsea where my cousin lived. How my heart thumped as I walked along the streets. My face was flushed, and I was in a state of intense excitement.

My cousin came to the door when I knocked.

"Bless me, Marion," she said. "What brings you here, child?" And she bent down and kissed me.

Seated on a footstool, with my head against her knee, I told her of my troubles and how I longed to get away from my grandmother and to earn a living.

"You poor kiddie," she said when I had finished, and began to sob quietly. "It's a queer job pretending to be your mother, but I don't mind risking it to help you.... You've had a cruel time of it, poor child. But it's a queer life that you're going into. It's hard work, and it's dangerous. You'll have to risk your life and limbs every time you perform, and the pay isn't very good. Have you thought of all this?"

"I'll do anything rather than go home," I said, pressing her hand eagerly.

"Very well, I'll come along with you," returned my cousin. "Just help yourself to some bread and jam while I get my things on."

I was glad to have something to eat, for I was very hungry; indeed, as I have said before, I knew the feeling of hunger only too well in those days.

Presently my cousin and I set out for Balham. We rode on an omnibus, and were soon at Mademoiselle Elvierra's lodgings.

The acrobat seemed pleased at seeing me back again so quickly. Turning to my cousin, she said: " She's a dear little child. She'll get on well with me."

" I hope so," my cousin said, pretending that she felt the parting from me very deeply. " I do hope she'll be a good girl. You'll look after her, won't you, and see that she always gets enough to eat ? "

" Of course, she'll be well treated. Don't you fear about that."

" Is it very dangerous ? " asked my cousin.

" Oh, dear no; nothing like what people think," said the artiste, smiling. " We teach all the tricks with a lunge, and our pupils never hurt themselves.

A DANCING GIRL

Even the trapeze and rings are not as dangerous as they look."

"Well, Marion, you've quite made up your mind?" asked my cousin.

"Oh, yes," I answered earnestly.

Mademoiselle Elvierra then produced a written contract, and began to fill in my name. She handed my cousin the pen. A glance of hesitation crossed her face for an instant, but she wrote her name hurriedly, and then, catching me in her arms, pressed me to her breast and kissed me long and lovingly. I do not think that the tears in her eyes were a pretence; they were real tears, for she felt deeply for me.

"It's always a sad business parting," said Mademoiselle Elvierra. "By the way," she added suddenly, "hasn't she any better clothes than those?"

"This is my only frock," I explained.

"Well, she must have another. You'll agree that this is very shabby."

My kindly cousin offered at once to buy me another frock and a hat.

I knew that this dear soul could not well afford to buy me clothes. But she was full of love and sympathy.

After tea we went shopping, and I returned to my cousin's house, carrying a pretty dress and blouse and a hat with poppies on it. I felt very happy indeed; I had only one regret. There was a girl friend—the only one I had—living in Camden Town, and I longed to say good-bye to her.

The longing was so strong that I could not resist it, and my cousin, touched by my affection for my friend, encouraged me to go and say good-bye to her.

Little did I think what would happen. My cousin gave me my bus fare, and I started off, eager to tell my friend of the good luck that had come to me. I was beginning a new life; in fact, I felt that I was just beginning to live for the first time. I had a beautiful new dress and a lovely hat, and I was going to Liverpool with mademoiselle to be an acrobat. It was like a fairy story.

I felt my heart beating with joy. Now I was free, and I was going to see the world.

These were my thoughts as I sat on top of a bus in Hampstead Road. I had never felt more happy and excited in my whole life. Judge of my dismay when I suddenly saw my grandmother standing on the pavement looking up at me. I realized at once that she had seen me. There was no escaping her. I sat stiff with fright; I didn't even attempt to get off the vehicle when it stopped. My heart stood still as my grandmother came up the steps to the bus roof. She just seized my arm and led me along. I was paralysed with fright; I couldn't speak a word.

Gripping my hand hard, she strode along to our home, and all she said was: "My word, you'll get it for this. You'll not run away again!"

When we reached home my grandmother's anger blazed up like a flame. She had restrained her temper in the street, but safely within the house, she lost all control, and began to rave.

"Look at her," she cried to my grandfather. "There's a disreputable child for you. She's too wicked for words. I'll teach you to run away." And with these words she struck me a severe blow in the face. I lay for an instant half-stunned. Then the wrathful woman seized me by the arm, and gave me a sound thrashing, finally dragging me to my bedroom and flinging me in.

I heard the key turn in the lock. I was a prisoner. My back was stiff and sore from the beating. But what hurt me most was the thought that I was locked up, and that Mademoiselle Elvierra was expecting me the next day. What would she think? I thought, too, of my cousin. She would be alarmed at my absence.

Oh, how I suffered that night! I cried and cried till my eyes ached. My position seemed quite hopeless; there was a hard fate against me. At the very moment when I fancied that I was free this terrible fate had overtaken me, and I was again in the clutch of my grandmother. I saw the dawn break, and I still lay sobbing on the bed in the utmost dejection.

It was Sunday morning, and the street was quiet. I could only hear the clink of the milkman's pail, the steady tread of a policeman, and the distant sound of a railway train. I knew that my guardians would not get up until about eleven o'clock.

A DANCING GIRL

Presently I became wild and desperate. I looked into the street, and measured with my eye the height of the drop on to the pavement. Had I been a trained acrobat, as I am now, I would not have hesitated to clamber down the water spout. But my courage was not strong enough to risk a broken neck. I wrung my hands in utter misery. Oh, that I could screw up my courage to leap out of the window. Again and again I looked down on the pavement with a shudder of fright. If I jumped and broke my leg, I could not get to Balham. No, fate was against me. I was a wretched, helpless little girl.

Soon I began to hear sounds in the house. My grandmother was up and getting a cup of tea to carry to my grandfather. The church bells began to ring, and people passed along the street. It was a bright day, and the sky was a clear blue, but the sunshine seemed to mock at my grief.

Suddenly the door was thrown open, and my stern grandmother appeared.

" Now, then, you worthless little hussy,

go and take the milk in, and then make your bed," she said, scowling at me.

Here was my chance. If I gained the front door I could easily make a dash down the street. My heart began to throb hurriedly, and my breath came short, as I opened the front door. The street was quiet; no one was in sight. I left the door open, darted off as fast as I could run, and flew round the first corner. In a few minutes I was panting down the Camden Road, running as I had never run before. Several people stared at me as I tore along. I think I ran nearly the whole length of the Hampstead Road before I dropped into a walk. I was at last forced to walk, for there was a sharp pain in my chest, and my breath was quite spent. But I am sure that I ran almost all the way to Balham. Sometimes I looked anxiously behind me, fearing that some one might be pursuing me. And when I thought of my grandmother's rage, I started to run again, like a hunted creature.

At last I staggered up the steps of Mademoiselle Elvierra's lodgings. I had scarcely strength enough left to knock at the door.

My future mistress was up and busy packing her things in a theatrical dress-basket. I entered a littered room, and found her, with her yellow hair down her back, kneeling at a drawer.

"Great Scott!" she exclaimed; "I've been tearing my hair all the morning. Do you know we're due at Euston in two hours? Where have you been? I expected you early."

Her voice was agitated and angry, and there was a gleam in her eyes that frightened me. I noticed that she was not a woman to be trifled with.

Well, I am afraid I told her a long string of fibs about having overslept myself, and lost my way walking from my cousin's house.

"You'll have to smarten up," she said. "If you'd have come a little later you'd have found me gone, bag and baggage, and you wouldn't have been able to find me. Where are those clothes you were going to get, and where is your hat?"

Then I remembered that I had run

away without my hat, and that my new clothes were at my cousin's.

"I'm sorry," I stammered. "You see, I was in such a hurry that I came out without my hat and the parcel of things."

"You little idiot," said Mademoiselle Elvierra. "We'll have to drive round that way and fetch your things. That'll be another two or three shillings for the cab fare. How vexing!"

She tossed a pair of mauve tights into the basket, and muttered something under her breath, which I took for a threat. It was quite plain that my employer had a temper. I wondered if I had jumped out of the frying-pan into the fire. Would she be cruel to me?

Soon the packing was finished, and I was sent to bring a four-wheeler from a neighbouring stand. Mademoiselle Elvierra was ready for the journey. Her cheeks were touched with rouge, and she had darkened her eyebrows, and passed a powder-puff over her face. She looked every inch a performer. No one could have mistaken her for anything else than a " professional." She wore a large, showy hat and a lot of flash jewellery.

I felt very shabby and insignificant by her side as we sat in the jolting cab.

At my cousin's I jumped out and rang the bell. Mademoiselle Elvierra remained in the cab, and told me to be quick.

My dear cousin was delighted to see me again, for she had been very alarmed at my absence; but there was no time to waste. I told my story hurriedly, took my clothes, and, after she had pressed me to her breast, and asked me to write often to her, my cousin bade me good-bye.

CHAPTER II

APPRENTICED TO AN ACROBAT

MADEMOISELLE ELVIERRA was booked for a week at a music-hall near Liverpool. We travelled to the North on Sunday with a number of other performers who were going to Lancashire, and we went to cheap lodgings in Liverpool. On the Monday morning I attended my first rehearsal. I was rather proud, for I was now " in the profession "; and I held my head up, and felt quite a little woman as I stood on the stage in the dim hall and watched my instructress climb up a rope to a fixed trapeze high up in the " flies."

She was in her practising dress, a sort of bathing costume; and her face was not made-up, as it was at night.

Sitting on the bar, Mademoiselle Elvierra drew her hands down a wet handkerchief suspended from one of the wire supports, and then began her evolutions, while the band played a slow, soft waltz. My mistress was a proficient gymnast. She was brought up to the business, and had performed in all parts of the United Kingdom and the Continent. And as I watched her I could not fail to admire her nerve, strength, and grace as she revolved on the bar, swung, hung by her heels, and finally performed a difficult trick of balancing while she lay with the small of her back on the trapeze.

"I shall have to learn all this," I thought to myself; and I felt somewhat frightened, for the trapeze was a great height above the stage, and there was no net under it to catch the artiste should she fall.

After practising her bar business, my mistress had a turn at the flying rings. She swung on the long cords, twisted and contorted her agile body, and flying from one pair of rings, caught another in mid-air. Her "number" lasted about ten minutes, and was very exciting.

From that day I began my apprenticeship of hard work. Every morning, clad in practice tights, and with gymnastic shoes on my feet, I learned hand-springs and somersaults on the stage. The hand-springs I soon mastered, for I was nimble; but the somersaults gave me a lot of trouble. It requires considerable nerve to turn a complete somersault without touching the ground with the hands. This feat cannot be learned without the help of the lunge, an apparatus which I had better explain. The lunge is a belt worn round the waist, and attached to the belt is a cord, which is fastened to a ring that runs along a wire stretched across the stage. Two assistants each hold cords fixed to the belt, and when the beginner gives the signal they jerk him over and help him to turn the somersault. It was with great delight that I found, one day, that I no longer required the lunge. I could turn a real, clean somersault by myself. Mademoiselle Elvierra was very pleased, and she rewarded me with sweets.

My first trials on the rings and the trapeze cost me some fear, and I shed tears now and then, when my teacher lost her temper, and called me a " little stupid " or " a fumblefist."

Apprentices to acrobats often have a very hard time. I do not accuse the mass of trainers of cruelty to the children entrusted to their care; but in this profession, as in all others, there are some men and women who show little consideration for their young pupils. I have seen children of tender years severely flogged for clumsiness in performing difficult gymnastic feats. Too often an impatient trainer resorts to the cane or the leather belt as a means of punishment. I have known cases of apprentices having been kicked by the teachers when in a passion. In one company with which I was associated there were two acrobats—a youth of twenty and his little brother of about ten. The young man treated the child most cruelly. He used to beat the boy across the shoulders, and I have seen the little fellow stiff and bruised from these thrashings with a stick. If anyone remonstrated with the elder brother he always replied: " Do you keep this boy, or do I ? Mind your own business."

A worse case was that of a performer, a foreigner, who had trained two little children—almost babies, a boy and a girl—in ground tumbling. This man was like a fiend.

It would be absurd to deny that there is a certain amount of rough treatment used in the training of children for the circus and the stage. But I am not making an attack on the trainers as a whole. Some of them are exceedingly fond of children, and display great patience in teaching them their tricks. There are hasty-tempered and unfeeling persons in every calling, and acrobatism is not an exception to the rule.

Mademoiselle Elvierra was not a very patient trainer, and I had several drubbings from her during my apprenticeship. As I grew older and bigger she showed less feeling for me, and her treatment was occasionally harsh. But, on the whole, I do not blame my instructress; she turned me into a capable child-performer in a very short time, and I was able to obtain engagements after we parted company.

After learning somersaults and ground tumbling, I began to practise on the fixed trapeze and the rings, and finally I became expert on the flying trapeze. Many were the headaches that I endured after spinning round and round on the bar, and very often my hands were so sore and blistered that the bar felt like red-hot iron.

The acrobat is continually in danger. A belt or a stay may give at any moment, and the apparatus and the artiste fall to the ground. Before I met with my one serious accident I had several tumbles, and I was always more or less bruised during my training. It is very trying to the nerves to mount up above the glittering lights of the stage, to swing on the trapeze, and to let go for a fly through the air. I used to suffer from nervousness at times, which almost paralysed me. In a flying trapeze act, in which one performer hangs by the legs from a bar, and catches the other performer by the hands as he flies to him through the air, it is most necessary that the nerves shall be steady and cool. The aim of the flying artiste must be good, and he must avoid a too rapid or a too slow flight.

The performer who catches him by the arms must be strong, with quickness and dexterity and perfect control of the nerves. It is a feat that always wins a round of applause, or, as we say in the business, " a good hand."

It was weeks before I felt quite confident on the flying trapeze. Even during years after the conclusion of my training, there were times when I felt quite nervous. The public do not realize that the smiling performer in her tights and her spangles may be suffering from a headache or neuralgia. Often I have endured agonies of faceache while performing my "number," and sometimes I have been quite ill and not fit for work. Think, too, of the ordeal of performing and appearing to enjoy it when the heart is heavy with sorrow, through domestic trouble or the loss of a relative! The life of the acrobatic artistes is not all excitement and pleasure; it is frequently very hard and trying, and at all times precarious.

To a nervous, inexperienced performer the clash and clatter of the orchestra is often irritating. I used to find that the music, especially if in waltz time, distracted my attention from my work, and made me somewhat careless; but I learned in time to forget it, and to go through my business without hearing the band.

When I travelled with Mademoiselle Elvierra there was no safety-net stretched under the trapeze, and the risk to life and limb was therefore high. One acrobat I knew on one occasion became suddenly dizzy, and, missing her hold after a flight, fell against a wire stay in her descent, and was caught by a hook, which entered her face. The marks of the wound are still on her cheek, and will remain until her dying day. Sprains, bruises, and blisters are quite common among acrobats, but serious accidents are not very frequent in the profession.

Looking back on these early days, I recall some happy times. We were always on the move, and I liked the constant change of scene. I had enough to eat; I was warmly clad in winter, and in the day-time, after practice, I did as I liked, and wandered about the towns that we visited. On the hoardings I saw the gaudy posters depicting " Mademoiselle Elvierra and Little Marion in their daring aerial act on the trapeze and flying rings." In the picture I appeared as a very small child, with a baby face, but it was not a good portrait of me.

We " worked " the smaller music-halls for a year or so, visiting London once or twice, where I appeared at the suburban variety shows.

In the country we performed in the Midlands and at Halifax, Wakefield, and other manufacturing towns. Several times we appeared at open-air fêtes during the summer months. My first Continental tour was with Mademoiselle Elvierra. I remember my excitement at seeing the sea for the first time, and the delight of going aboard a vessel bound for Holland. It was a new and thrilling experience. We performed first in Amsterdam, and then moved on to Rotterdam, where we were booked for the celebrated La Scala Theatre.

At Rotterdam my teacher and I fell out seriously. I was a very sensitive child, and though I do not think I am a coward, I always felt the indignity of a whipping very acutely. I could be led by kindness, but harshness always made me rebellious. Well, at the La Scala my mistress beat me for some trifling mistake, and I took the punishment very much to heart. In a moment of impulse and misery I went into the street, resolved that I would never return again to Mademoiselle Elvierra. I turned up the main street of the city, my heart aching, and my eyes blinded with tears; and as I walked I repeated, " I'll never go back. I'll never go back."

A feeling of dread came over me as I walked about the streets of the city of Rotterdam. What would become of me? I realized that I was quite alone in the world, and what can a child of twelve do in such a plight? The thought that I was bound body and soul to Mademoiselle Elvierra filled me with despair. I was her property; she could treat me as she chose.

After roaming about for hours in this strange city, among people whose language I could not understand, I felt my fear increasing. If I had possessed any money I would have gone back to England; but I was quite penniless and helpless. The feeling of freedom gave me no happiness; for I could not think what would become of me in this strange land. And as the day wore on, and I grew tired of wandering, I realized that I had made a mistake in running away.

Towards evening, feeling faint with

hunger, I sat down in a public garden. Tears came into my eyes. How I longed for a mother to whom I could turn in my trouble. But there was no one in the world who cared for me. While these sad thoughts filled my mind I saw a man in uniform approaching me. He stopped as he came near the seat, and looked me in the face. Then he put his hand on my shoulder, and said something that I could not understand. He seemed vexed that I did not understand his language, and, with impatience, he growled:

"Policeman, me."

That was all the English that he appeared to know. I was frightened when he caught hold of my arm and led me away. The passers-by stopped and stared; they thought that I was being arrested for stealing or some other crime. We walked through many streets, the policemen clutching my arm, till we came in sight of the Scala.

I knew then that I was being taken back to Mademoiselle Elvierra, and I began to sob and tremble. She had set the police on my track, and a search had been made for me. I knew that a severe punishment awaited me.

Mademoiselle was in her dressing-room, preparing for her turn. When we entered she was rouging her pale cheeks, and she turned round, with an angry glare in her eyes.

"You little wretch!" she cried. "So you thought you'd run away, did you? I'll teach you for this!"

The policeman took a tip which she handed to him, and with a bow left us alone. As soon as the door was closed my trainer rushed at me in a fury, and shook me violently. Then she seized a hairbrush, and beat me with it on the head and shoulders. I thought she would never stop; I felt sore and stunned as I sank to the floor. I was too dazed and scared to cry out; I just crouched in a corner, choking and moaning.

I covered my face with my hands, and prayed God to help me. I knew that I was utterly at the mercy of this woman, and that she could do as she pleased with me. My state of helplessness was terrible, and I groaned with despair.

Presently the acrobat passed the powder-puff over her face, and went to do her turn alone. For the first time I was not in the show, and I felt rather disappointed, for I liked the excitement of appearing before the audience.

I heard the applause that greeted my mistress at the conclusion of her trapeze performance, and then the door opened, and she came in, hot and rather out of breath. Instead of beating me again, as I expected, she sat down, fanned herself with her handkerchief, and then lit a cigarette. The applause had pleased her, and her face looked less angry. Beyond a long scolding, I received no more correction for running away.

Soon after this adventure we returned to England, and for a time we suffered ill-luck. One of the trials of the artiste is the uncertainty of engagements, and we were in for a spell of misfortune. Every day we called upon an agent. I can see him now; a stout man, with a cigar always between his puffy lips.

"Very sorry, my dear; nothing doing just now," was his answer day after day.

And with her teeth set, and a look of disappointment on her face, my mistress would walk silently back to our one room in Lambeth.

But one day the agent had good news for us. He said that a certain circus was starting for the Continent, and that a pair of female acrobats were required for about a year's tour. Mademoiselle Elvierra almost cried with joy. The salary was good, and she was very glad to get into work again with one of the best shows on the road. I was also delighted at the turn of our bad luck, and the thought of travelling again filled me with excitement. On the strength of this engagement, my trainer borrowed money, and bought new clothes for herself and for me. In a few days we started for Holland with the big circus. We seldom stayed more than a day at one town, and the work was pretty hard, for there were two performances daily. Often on the railway journeys I slept from sheer tiredness. But I enjoyed the life. We were well treated by the management, the pay was good and regular, and we had many pleasant days in the old towns of Germany, such as Berlin, Darmstadt, and Munich.

Every week I was getting more proficient in my business. I seldom experienced nervousness, and I was always proud when the spectators applauded my flights on the flying trapeze. I began to think of the days when I could command a good salary and perform by myself.

While I was with this circus I made friends with the company, and met many well-known artistes, equestrians, wire-walkers, clowns, and also made friends with the performing animals. I was especially interested in a performing troupe of dogs, and loved to play with them in the ring after their daily practice. During my career I have travelled with many kinds of animal shows, and watched the method of trainers.

There is a good deal of talk about the cruelty of showmen towards animals, but the charges are often exaggerated. Most animals cannot be trained by harshness. Horses, dogs, and cats are apt to become sulky if unkindly treated; and

A DANCING GIRL

I can assure my readers that, as a rule, more patience is shown in teaching animals than in training young children. If a dog is badly beaten he will mope in a corner, and no human power will force him to show his tricks. All animals have to be humoured and coaxed to perform, and they expect a reward of food after their show.

Performing birds are very apt to sulk, and it is always difficult to train them. Dogs, especially mongrels, learn rather quickly to perform if they are well-treated. Some animal showmen have wonderful power of training, and their success is due to patience, tact, and firmness.

I will not say that there is no cruelty connected with animal performances. The creatures that suffer the most are the wild ones in cages. Their life to me has always seemed very pitiable. But the public will flock to see these shows, and the trainers give the public what they want.

Lions in cages are sometimes so depressed that they almost lose their fierceness, and means are taken to make them ferocious. I have seen a certain lion-tamer flog his lions for no fault whatever, but simply to irritate them and make them roar and lash their tails and look furious. Some lions are fed on cooked meat, and these are the most easy to train and handle. But a lion-tamer who wishes his lions to appear savage gives them raw flesh and is unsparing in the use of the lash.

It is an interesting fact that animals have an ear for music. I have no doubt of this, for I have noticed it again and again in circus and music-hall shows in England and on the Continent.

Horses, dogs, elephants and lions are all able to distinguish the tunes that are played during their performances, and this is easily proved by watching the animals behind the scenes. A comedian may have just finished his turn when the music for a performing dog show strikes up. Immediately all the dogs in the troupe are excited. If any of them have been asleep, they wake up, begin to wag their tails and show real excite-

A DANCING GIRL

ment, often barking eagerly. The same interest in their music is shown by other animals, even by sea-lions.

Animals on the stage and in the circus ring are very proud of applause. They are quite as vain as the human performers, and show by their expression and their antics that they understand what the noise of hand-clapping really means. Performing animals often enjoy their work, and the stories that they are whipped on to the stage are exaggerated. As a rule, the animals are kept hungry before their performance, and they know that after the show they will have a good meal. Only those who live constantly among trained animals know how clever they become.

My German tour with the circus was not very eventful until we reached Magdeburg. At this town a serious misfortune befell me. I was going through my performance before a crowded house one night, when, for the first time, I met with a really bad accident. There is a trick on the hand-rings called the "splits." It is not a very elegant feat, but it is one that most artistes learn, and the public seem to like it. This trick always gave me some trouble in balancing, and upon this occasion one of my feet slipped in the ring, and before I could regain my balance I fell into the arena. I remember hearing a thud as I fell from the rings; then darkness came over me, and I was unconscious. I heard afterwards that there were cries of sympathy from the audience. Mademoiselle Elvierra ran forward and picked me up, and I was carried out.

CHAPTER III

LIFE IN THE PROFESSION

WHEN I was carried out of the ring senseless and injured, it was feared that my fall was likely to be fatal. I cannot remember all that immediately followed my accident. When I became conscious I was in the public hospital, and surgeons and nurses were attending to my injuries. I had dislocated my right arm; I was considerably bruised, and had much internal pain. For eight weeks I lay in bed, kindly treated by every one, and it was nearly three weeks more before I was considered fit to return to my work. Meantime, the circus had visited many towns in Germany, and Mademoiselle Elvierra was performing alone.

One day, when I was almost well, a nurse told me that an English young lady wished to see me. She had heard that one of her country-women was ill, and she thought I might be pleased to see her. I was very glad to look again upon an English face and to hear my own language spoken. But I was a little surprised when a fair-haired girl, in the uniform of the Salvation Army, came to my bedside. It seemed strange to encounter a Salvationist in Magdeburg.

"Well, my sister," said the lieutenant, taking my hand, "I hope you are getting well, and that you are out of pain. I have come to read the Bible to you."

Then she opened the book and began to read, and after reading a chapter from the Gospels, she inquired into my religious belief. As I have said, I was brought up in the Roman Catholic creed. But to this good soul my religion seemed worse than no religion at all. She was very concerned, too, that a girl of my age should be in the acrobatic profession.

"It is not a proper occupation for a girl," said my visitor. "You can't serve God and the world, and your business is full of danger to the soul."

"But many in the profession are very religious," I said.

However, the Salvation lass would not agree that a good life can be lived by anyone on the stage. She used rather strong language in describing the immorality of artistes.

And now that I am referring to this question, I will take the opportunity of telling the truth about the alleged wickedness of variety and circus performers. Believe me, my readers, we are not nearly so "immoral" as we are painted. If a girl wishes to live a straight life on the stage it is in her power to do so.

I do not deny that there are certain

temptations in the professional life. Is there any calling for women free from temptation? It may seem strange to some of my readers, yet it is a fact that very many dancers and acrobats are quite respectable women; not only so, but many of them are strait-laced and prudish.

It is often said that a woman who wears scanty clothing or tights in public must have lost all sense of modesty. This is an absurd error. A man who wears a handsome uniform does not necessarily become as vain as a peacock. The airy costume of the ballet dancer and the tights of the principal boy in pantomime are conventions, and the artiste looks upon them very much as a soldier or a postman regards his uniform. Many artistes do not admire the popular fashion in these matters, but the managers, the costumiers and the wardrobe mistresses know that the public expect the dancer or the acrobat to wear tights, and the artiste must comply with the public taste. I have seen trapeze performers in frocks, and I certainly think that gymnastic tights are more suitable and decent than skirts.

People who are ready to see evil in the life of the stage and the ring believe any story that is told them about chorus girls and acrobats and their manners and customs. There is a certain amount of Bohemianism and freedom in the profession, but the " vice " has been grossly exaggerated. A gymnast must be a sober liver, or his nerves will soon go to pieces, and, as a matter of fact, most acrobatic artistes indulge quite moderately in alcoholic drinks, while some are strict teetotallers.

One artiste with whom I travelled for six months was undoubtedly a heavy drinker. He ran a troupe, and his wife was a member of it. We did some very daring aerial feats on the trapeze, and I used to make flights while he hung head downwards waiting to grip my hands. I don't know how I lived through that time of horror. For six months I never flew from the trapeze without dreading an accident, for I knew that this man had been drinking all day, and that he was never quite sober. His wife often declared that my fears were quite foolish. She said that her husband always knew what he was doing in spite of his intemperate habits. But night after night I expected a bad fall, and I never felt confident while I was performing with this troupe.

While defending the profession against the too frequent and ill-founded charges of drunkenness and immorality, I do not wish to go to extremes and pretend that there are no black sheep in the flock. I have, of course, seen instances of girls coming to trouble through folly or vanity, and I have met men on the stage who squander their salaries in drink and gambling. But performers are not all either black or white; there are all sorts of men and women in the world behind the scenes.

I must now return to the Salvation Army lieutenant and her visits to me while I was in the hospital at Magdeburg. This kind-hearted but rather narrow-minded girl made me promise that I would attend one of her meetings as soon as I was well enough to walk. I promised to do this, and she seemed pleased, for she had a great desire to make me a convert and to persuade me from continuing in what she called "a sinful life." Therefore, one day I attended a meeting of the Army, and was given a seat in the front row. I soon learnt that it was a special occasion. A number of the "soldiers" had come in the expectation that I would stand up and make a startling confession and announce that I intended leaving the stage for ever. Prayers were offered up for me, and I was invited by one officer after another to join the Army. But I have my own convictions about religion, and I refused.

The lieutenant pleaded very earnestly with me that evening, using every argument she could to induce me to abandon the profession. Poor young woman, she was very sincere, and I felt grateful for her coming to comfort me in the hospital. But I could not join the Army. For one thing, I was still serving my apprenticeship to Mademoiselle Elvierra.

"You won't leave the company of sinners, then?" said the girl sadly.

"I shall never forget your kindness," I said awkwardly.

"Ah, it is terrible to think that you will be lost."

And with these words the lieutenant pressed my hand, and amid the murmur of voices I went from the barracks.

A few days after this I joined Mademoiselle Elvierra at Hanover.

Travelling with a tenting circus is not unenjoyable during a fine summer; but in wet weather there are many hardships connected with the life. When two performances are given a day, the artiste is worked very hard, and much of his spare time is spent in the train. If his turn is finished at ten o'clock at night, he goes to bed, sleeps for a few hours, and then catches a train for the next town. At midday he may be expected to ride in the "parade" or procession through the streets, and at two o'clock he must begin to dress for the afternoon performance. This means pretty constant work during the twenty-four hours of each week day. How welcome is the Sunday rest! But on the Continent the artiste is expected to work quite as hard on Sundays as on weekdays, and this makes a Continental engagement very trying. At the same time every performer is glad to be in " a shop," no matter how hard the work, for in the profession every one dreads those terrible and depressing periods when leisure is not a matter of choice but of necessity.

On the whole I enjoyed my circus career, and especially after the termination of my apprenticeship, when I was able to command a fair salary. My trainer is, I believe, still on the road, and the last time I heard of her was in America. Soon after I left her she married an acrobat, and they performed a trapeze act together.

Upon returning to England, after my travels with the circus, I went to see some of my friends. I was especially glad to see my cousin again, the kind woman who had impersonated my mother, and signed the contract for me with Mademoiselle Elvierra. But for her, I might never have obtained work as an acrobat.

For a time I was "resting," and prospects looked rather gloomy. My lodging bills began to eat up my little savings and my clothes were getting shabby.

Oh! those are grey days, when the artiste awakes in the morning with the reflection that the last shilling has been spent, and that the chances of getting into work are very meagre. This is a dark side of the performer's life, and the public little know how some of us suffer. Even the " star," who can ask a high salary, has ups and downs, and is sometimes forced to borrow money on his contracts. There is a class of moneylenders who advance money to artistes. The interest is tremendous, as the risk is said to be great; but if the moneylender holds the contract as security, there is not much danger that he will lose his money. I have known performers who have paid as much as sixty per cent interest for loans during bad times. The principal and interest have to be paid as soon as the artiste gets into work again, and this is a fearful drain upon the salary.

The fact is there are too many people in the equestrian and variety professions, and too many regular actors on the regular stage. For acrobats, except a few of the more noted and fortunate, the outlook nowadays is far from cheerful. The days of the circus in England are almost over. The music-halls have practically killed the circus. Many acrobats, and even equestrians, depend nowadays upon the halls, for there are so few circuses on the road.

What has become of the clown who used to delight audiences in the manufacturing towns and the country villages in the days of the travelling circus? The number grows fewer every year, and some of the survivors are now doing their business on the variety halls.

It may be said that with the enormous increase of the number of music-halls there ought to be plenty of openings for artistes of all kinds. There are splendid chances, no doubt, for brilliant comedians and comic singers, and for all sorts of novel turns; but without striking originality, the beginner must prepare himself for a life of continual disappointment. Although there are ten times as many " variety palaces," " empires " and " hippodromes " as there were in the days of my apprenticeship, it is still difficult to get regular employment. The public hear that a performer is earning £10 a week, and they think it is a noble salary for about two hours' work each evening. Thousands of girls employed in shops and factories think that the life of the gymnast or the dancer is a very easy one, and that the pay is splendid compared with their own earnings.

The artiste's salary would be fairly good if it was regular. But it is very rarely regular. At least fifty out of every hundred performers are unable to get engagements for more than six months in the year. A large proportion of artistes only work for a month or two in the year. This is not always because they are incompetent, but because the profession is overcrowded. There is no trouble nowadays for the manager who wishes to get a variety company together. He can command fair talent for very little money.

Have you ever seen the crowd of anxious-looking women and girls waiting at the stage door of a theatre when the management has advertised for chorus ladies, or for show ladies to " walk on " in musical comedies or dramas? Have you ever seen a throng of expectant girls before the rehearsals of pantomimes, standing in the cold and rain at the dingy doors of the suburban or East-end theatres? More than once have I been in one of those crowds. One by one the aspirants for stage glory go before the bluff stage-manager, who is often too harassed and busy to appear polite or sympathetic. "Let me try your voice. Where's your music?"

The trembling girl begins to sing at the piano. Perhaps by the end of the first verse the manager holds up his hand, and says, "Thanks; that will do. I'm afraid you can't sing well enough. Next one, please."

With an aching heart and tears in her eyes, the poor rejected chorus girl goes into the street, longing to hide her face from every one.

What an ordeal, too, is a "trial show" at one of the big music-halls. Your agent has arranged that you shall give your performance before the managing directors of the hall at some time between eleven and one o'clock in the morning. It is a big and important hall, and if you pass the trial you may get booked for this show and for all the halls belonging to the syndicate. You are full of hope, but terribly nervous. The night before the trial performance you cannot sleep. You keep repeating over and over in your mind: " I wonder if I shall be right ? "

The morning finds you anxious and excited. You cannot eat your breakfast, and as you walk to the hall your heart beats fast. If you have an elaborate wardrobe and " props " you have to pay for a cab.

When you enter the theatre you find a crowd of artistes of all sorts on the stage. Some are already dressed and made up to go on. Every one looks nervous. There is no joking or laughter; the performers talk in low tones in corners. In the dressing-room a number of girls and women are making up their faces. There is a faded woman, with dyed hair, trying to impart to her worn cheeks the bloom and attraction of youth with the aid of rouge, eyebrow pencils, and powder.

There are young girls who have never appeared on the stage. Some of these are in an agony of nervous fear, while others are absurdly confident of success. The room is overcrowded and close. There is a smell of grease paints and powder. One girl has forgotten her rouge; another has to run out and buy safety pins. A shy amateur, with stage aspirations, feels very out of place here, and looks exceedingly uncomfortable in her costume. The "old hands" are soon ready for the turn, and they go on the dark stage, and sit on any box or seat that is lying about the place. Meanwhile the stage-manager is writing down names:

"Miss Nicely—are you there?"

The young lady, clad in the tights and jewels of the "principal boy," comes forward, smiling.

"You go on third, remember," says the stage-manager. "Where are the Brothers Sleight?"

Two knockabout comedians, in red wigs and quaint attire, answer to the name. Then the gas is turned on and the footlights glitter, and, peeping from the wings, you see the directors taking their places in the stalls. They are a very ordinary collection of English gentlemen, well-dressed and mostly elderly; but they appear awfully imposing, like a row of stern judges. Sometimes there is no orchestra present, and the singers are accompanied by a pianist. The first turn is perhaps a conjurer; he is followed by a comic singer, and then I go on with three other girls, and we give our acrobatic "number." It is a terrible time. There is no applause, not a sign of approval from the keen-eyed gentlemen in the stalls. We come off, hot and panting, wondering whether we have satisfied the directors. I peep from the wings, and see the gentlemen talking about us. How I long to know our fate! But we may not hear for a few days, and meanwhile we are on tenterhooks of anxiety.

These trial shows are trials in more senses than one. Sometimes there are thirty turns on the list, and as the time is limited, the unfortunate artistes are told, as they go on the stage, "Only two minutes for your turn," or "Only one song, please."

The artiste is bewildered. He expected that he would be allowed five minutes at least. He almost forgets his words, and when he begins to sing, he may realize that he is out of time, and that his nervousness is evident. Even a good artiste may appear to great disadvantage at one of these trial performances. I would rather face any audience than go before a board of directors at a trial show.

At a certain music-hall, the custom of giving a performer a "raspberry" was not uncommon, and this custom prevails in some of the halls in the North of England. A "raspberry" may be a jeering noise when an artiste is singing or dancing, a cat-call, a cuckoo-cry, or a shrill derisive whistling. Sometimes the artistes are treated to such comments as this: "Sing up, old ginger-hair," "Give it a lift," "My word, he nearly burst his wind-pipe with that note!" and so on. If the artiste shows annoyance or anger he will get more "raspberries," and possibly a " bird " into the bargain. " Getting the bird " is the worst that can happen to a performer at a trial or any other show. In plain English, " getting the bird " means being hissed. I suppose that term comes from the hissing noise that some birds, such as geese, make when they are angry. It may be said that the " bird " is sometimes deserved by the artiste. But whether it is merited or not, it means very often that the artiste is doomed, for no manager can stand hissing from an audience.

Ordinary chaff among the audience may do an artiste good, if he keeps his temper and tries to return it. I once saw Chirgwin, the White-eyed Kaffir, "guyed" by some young gentlemen in a box at the London Pavilion. Chirgwin let them amuse themselves for a time, then he pointed to the box and said: " What! Only one bottle of ginger ale among three of you, and yet you're so merry!" The roar that came from the audience quite disconcerted the young men in the box, and they ceased their attempts at giving " raspberries."

At one hall in the East of London, where public trial performances are given on one afternoon a week, the audience is a very lively one, and quick to detect any point that gives the opportunity for chaff. So rough is the banter here that many artistes dread the hall, and it is said that only by luck can one escape a " raspberry " or " the bird."

My career as an aerial acrobat was full of trials and dangers, but I do not regret that I served my time as an apprentice to this calling. The constant physical exercise was good for my health while I was growing, and my trapeze work taught me agility, quickness, and " nerve." I am sure that my gymnastics have been of use to me as a dancer.

But I did not wish to remain always the member of an acrobatic troupe. I began to grow more and more interested in stage dancing during my first Continental tour, and soon the desire to become a dancer was very strong. I think dancing is far more graceful and pretty than acrobatics. Some of the gymnastic contortions that the public seem to admire are to my mind far from pleasing. There is no grace in the tricks of a "bender" or "contortionist," but in the case of a skilful dancer every movement may be delightful to the eye of the spectators.

I am now coming to that period of my life when I resolved to learn stage dancing. I did not abandon gymnastics altogether. There have been times when I have returned for a while to the old business on the trapeze, flying rings, and horizontal bars; but I do not now describe myself as a gymnastic artiste.

In the next chapter I shall relate a few experiences of the acrobat's life, and then begin to write the story of my early dancing days in all parts of Europe.

CHAPTER IV

HOW I BECAME A DANCER

THE next engagement that I obtained was with an acrobatic troupe. Our agent booked us for the Moss-Stoll tour, and opened at the London Hippodrome, where we showed for four weeks. This was my first appearance in one of the big London variety palaces, though I had performed often in minor halls.

With this combination I performed at the Shepherd's Bush Empire, Hackney Empire, Holloway Empire, New Cross Empire, Cardiff, Swansea, Newport, Nottingham, Leicester, Manchester, Edinburgh, Glasgow, Hull, and several other towns.

My impressions of audiences may interest my readers. Let me say that in my business I have usually found that the provincial audiences are more appreciative than those of London. Some artistes speak of the roughness of the Lancashire and Yorkshire folk; but in the manufacturing towns of the North of England I have met with much kindness. The people of the North expect a good show for their money, but they are unstinting in applause when a turn pleases them.

The coldest audience I have ever faced was to be seen in Glasgow. I do not say that the Scotch are always undemonstrative, but they do not often applaud with the heartiness and enthusiasm of the southerners. I have referred to the custom of " guying " a performer and giving him what is called a " raspberry." Not a few artistes have had " raspberries " from the audiences in the Glasgow variety halls.

The success of the Sisters was so assured that a manager in Berlin wired for us to go there upon the termination of our contract with the Moss-Stoll company. This was my second visit to Germany, and I saw again many of the towns where I had performed with Mademoiselle Elvierra in my circus days.

By this time I was quite proficient as a flying trapeze artiste. I never experienced the least nervousness, and it was of no importance to me whether I performed with or without a safety-net. I am actually more nervous when crossing the crowded streets of London than I am when I am flying from one trapeze to another, or balancing myself in the flying rings, twenty feet or more above the ground.

My dancing days began with eight

hours' practice a day with a class at a dancing school in London. I was determined to learn my new profession as quickly as possible, for I wanted to be earning money. Having very little money in reserve, it was a strain upon my small savings to pay for lessons.

There are many kinds of stage dancing, but a majority of dancers specialize in one or two styles of dancing. I tried to learn as many styles as I could, and I have now a long list of dances in which I am proficient. I have several note-books full of directions as to the various steps in dances, written down from time to time, with a number of fresh steps and poses.

The ordinary stage dances as seen in England are classed as buck, or clog, jink shoe, sand dances, eccentric, acrobatic and skirt dances. Then there are the skipping-rope, graceful dances, hornpipes, reels, and big-boot dances. In time I mastered all the ordinary step-dances performed by variety artistes, and I also learned many of the ballet steps and the pirouette. Perhaps it will be well if I explain the different sorts of dances. The usual step-dance, in stage clogs, with jingles or " jinks " on the heels, is popular everywhere. The beginner finds the shuffling movement of the feet and the double taps with the heels a very complicated and difficult matter. I have seen girls cry with vexation because they found the steps so difficult to master.

The sand dance is of American origin, like the cake-walk, the two-step and several other eccentric dances. Sand-dancing is really dexterous shuffling of the feet to music, and to increase the sound made by the feet the stage is strewn with sand.

There are acrobatic and eccentric dances without number, and every performer in this line has his own specialities, such as high-kicking and leg-twisting. The skirt-dance is fairly modern, and is often introduced into musical comedy and light opera. Graceful dances include the old-fashioned minuets, waltzes, and Spanish and Russian dances. There are hornpipes and reels of all sorts, from the simple sailor's hornpipe to the Highland fling and the strathspeys.

Descriptive dancing is now considered to be of the highest artistic order, and very clever people write learnedly of the dancing of such exponents as Maud Allan and her numerous imitators. This dancing is seen at its best in Russia, where the ballet is in the highest favour amongst the wealthy class. It is also popular in France and Spain. In Spain, as I soon learned, dancing is regarded quite seriously as a high art, and many of the dances of that country are of Moorish origin and very ancient.

I will not bore my readers with an essay upon dancing; but they will probably like to know how dancing is taught in the stage academies. In most of the schools where pupils are trained for the variety stage, dancing is taught in classes. Recently there has been a demand for troupes of girl dancers in all parts of Europe and in America and the Colonies. There is hardly a civilized country where you will fail to find a company of English dancers in one or another of the large towns.

Many girls begin their careers as

dancers by joining a troupe of six or eight. A favourite number is eight. The girls must be young and attractive as well as good dancers, and in most cases they must be able to sing. The girl who can sing well and knows music stands a much better chance of success in the troupe, or as a solo dancer, than the girl who has a poor sense of tune and time and a weak and unpleasing voice. A really good singer or dancer working a turn by herself is in a better position than a member of a troupe. In the dancing schools the hours are often from four to six hours a day. The exercise is very tiring at first. Perspiration streams down the dancers faces; their limbs ache and feel stiff after an hour or so, and the beginners often fall out of the row and sink into a chair quite exhausted. In the earliest stages, while simple steps are being learned, the pupil rests her hands on a bar that stretches across the room.

The dress is like a gymnastic costume, and dancing pumps or light leather clogs are worn. A pianist plays the air, at first slowly, but the music becomes livelier as the pupils advance in their tuition.

A large number of girls are seized with a craze for dancing. They come to the schools from all ranks of society, but most of them are from struggling families who find it hard to make both ends meet. One girl will show a natural gift for dancing as soon as she joins a class, while another is very slow in learning the simplest movements of the legs and positions of the body. Again and again I have seen girls sent away from troupes and combinations as quite incapable of keeping time and step.

Nowadays I often teach troupes and solo dancers, and I can tell almost at a glance whether a girl is teachable or not. I remember my own difficulty in mastering the art of dancing, and feel very sympathetic towards those who are slow and awkward. I came to the dancing school after a severe training as a lofty and a ground tumbler, and I was in excellent physical condition. A girl who begins to learn dancing after working in a milliner's shop, or at some sedentary employment, finds the work very hard indeed. Her muscles are soft, she has lost her childish agility, and her breathing power is feeble. After a long and complicated dance beginners often reel and stagger as though they would fall. But after training, the lungs grow stronger and the muscles become accustomed to the severe exertion.

In theatres and music-halls the dancers are often rewarded with an encore for their performance. Now, this is very gratifying to an artiste, for it shows that her dancing is admired. But to come on after a very trying dance is very exhausting work and a tremendous tax upon the dancer's strength. Sometimes an artiste feels like fainting after giving an encore dance. The public do not realize this. If they knew how severe is the demand on the dancer's strength, they might refrain from the encore. However, I do not think that dancers would like to see the encore abolished.

A number of society ladies learn graceful dancing in the theatrical schools, so that they may entertain their friends at private parties. These pupils are often difficult to teach. A lady thinks that because she is pretty and has a charming figure she ought to shine as a skirt-dancer; but there are other things besides looks and a shapely form that go to the making of an expert dancer. The heart and the lungs must be strong and the limbs supple, and the dancer must have a sense of music and a natural grace of movement.

When training for the pantomimes or the halls the artistes are worked very hard for weeks. A new dance must be practised daily until every step, gesture, pose and movement of the arms is perfect. In a troupe every dancer must work in time. It is necessary, too, that the dancers should be all of the same height. A troupe with two girls of about five feet and one or two of five feet eight inches would look ridiculous.

One of the popular dances that I have found most difficult is the skipping-rope dance. I cannot say why that is so, for there are more difficult dances. Hornpipes and step-dances, with clogs or jink shoes,

I soon mastered, as well as skirt and graceful dances. My acrobatic training was of great service to me in learning eccentric dances, in which the leg muscles play a very active part.

The dancer's life is not all bright and exciting. There is much patient, hard work connected with it, and the chances of even fair success are only moderate. I like my profession, and would not care to change it for another; but I do not wish to draw a too attractive picture of a stage dancer's life. No girl should enter into this profession unless she is prepared to work hard and to suffer disappointments and to wait patiently for success. There are too many dancers, as I have said before. But there are not too many really clever dancers, and the artiste who can think out a new line for herself as a solo dancer stands a fair chance of earning regular money. In some cases she may be able to secure a high salary.

The pay of dancers varies considerably. I have known girls who have earned as little as ten shillings a week, and that not regularly. Fifty shillings to three pounds a week, with travelling expenses, is considered a pretty good salary for a troupe dancer. Even an able solo dancer in the pantomimes at small theatres may not earn more than two pounds a week for two performances a day. I have known the manager of a touring comedy company to offer as little as thirty shillings a week to a dancer, and he had no trouble in finding an artiste to take the offer.

There are no fortunes to be made as a dancer unless you happen to be a Loie Fuller, a Genée, a Maud Allan, or a La Belle Otero. But most dancers of the rank and file like the stage life, and prefer it to business. They are doing the work they like, and this is a compensation for their small pay.

The salary of a dancer would be good when compared with that of a waitress, seamstress, or typist if the work were regular. But in the variety profession the work is not regular, except for a minority of exceptionally brilliant " stars." Two pounds a week for six months in the year only equals a pound a week taking the year through. A girl who can ask three pounds a week may think herself very well off—and so she is for the time being—compared with a shop assistant. But at any time the dancer may be suddenly thrown out of work. Her position after weeks of unemployment is very deplorable. I could tell many tales of the suffering that I have witnessed among artistes who were said to be " resting."

A dancer " out of a shop " must appear respectable. She must not wear shabby clothes or look broken down. When she interviews an agent or a manager she must wear a nice dress and hat, smile, and appear to be flourishing and happy. How can she accomplish this when she is in debt at her lodgings, underfed, and depressed in spirits? This is the riddle that one has to solve, for there must be no hint of failure written upon the face or stamped in the seedy dress and faded hat.

My début as a dancer was in a touring " combination company." We were booked for a tour in the small towns of the Midlands and the North of England. But trade was bad just then, and in some towns the audiences were small, and our manager soon found that his resources were quite exhausted.

In the fourth week of our tour we were stranded at the manufacturing town of Wednesbury. I shall never forget this experience, because it was the first of the kind. We had started out from London full of hope, and prospects seemed good. It was a good combination, with several clever variety artistes as members; and our " number " had been carefully practised for weeks. We had also obtained new stage costumes for this expedition.

A mishap of this sort is, unfortunately, common in the profession, and it is the frequent fate of small companies working town-halls and assembly-rooms with variety turns. When we were told that there was nothing in the treasury, and that salaries would not be paid that week, I felt that I could cry. So far as my memory serves me, we four girls had only a shilling or two amongst us. What were we to do in this predicament? We had not even the price of our fares back to London. It was a very serious position, for starvation was staring us in the face.

Well, every cloud has its silver lining. To our immense relief, some of the townsfolk rallied round us in our trouble, and a benefit performance was arranged in the town-hall. The show was fairly well attended, and we all worked with a will to please our audience. But when we came to receive our share of the takings we found that there was barely enough to pay our fares to London.

A time of hardship, anxiety and disappointment followed upon this fiasco in the Black Country. I had to endure the bitterness of " resting," when I had hoped that my position as a dancer was assured. I almost regretted that I had left the acrobatic business. Even in that line there were no vacancies anywhere. It was a period of despair.

But one day, to my utter delight, my agent informed me that he was sending out a troupe called the Six Turner Girls. The pay was not high, by any means, but it was enough to live upon. In a week we started for the Midlands, where we performed at Walsall, Bordesley, Leicester, West Bromwich and other towns.

A better chance turned up for me when I made the acquaintance of a Greek artiste named Gamboli. He had married a girl friend of mine, a clever dancer, and she was now the mother of a lovely boy of about three years of age. Lily Gamboli had been my close friend, and when her husband proposed that I should join them and go to France, I seized at the chance of travelling in such congenial company.

Mr Gamboli is one of the cleverest artistes with whom I have been associated. He is full of ideas for novel " numbers," he has artistic feeling and is well educated. He is fluent in several languages, and has much tact and business capacity.

With the Gambolis I went to Paris. It was my first visit to this beautiful city, and I shall never forget how it delighted me. What a contrast it was here in the tree-shaded streets and charming gardens to the dingy manufacturing towns of England! It seemed like a new world.

We opened in Paris at the famous Folies Bergère, a splendid hall of the first class, where we posed in various living statue groups, besides performing several dances. Our show was a success, and our reputation spread from hall to hall. We performed successfully at the Casino de Paris and at several of the leading *café chantants* for several months.

This was a prosperous time, and I was very happy with my friends, the Gambolis. We all three worked well together, and put our hearts into our " numbers." This pleasant time in Paris was followed by a no less enjoyable series of engagements in Switzerland. For a month we made good money in Geneva, and we visited other towns before returning to delightful Paris.

I do not wish to appear ungrateful to my own countrymen, but I am bound to say that the artiste is better treated, in almost every sense, on the Continent than he is in our country. The British public are not unkindly on the whole; but in England the performer is often regarded with mingled scorn and pity as a lazy person and a ne'er-do-well and " waster." Of course, the public have their pets in the profession; but the mass of artistes are often spoken of, with a shrug of the shoulders, as " those music-hall people!" Even many actors on the "legitimate" stage often express contempt for the variety artistes.

It is different on the Continent. I have performed, both as an acrobat and a dancer, in Holland, Belgium, France, Germany, and Spain, and everywhere I have met with courtesy and kindness. A French or a Spanish manager is almost invariably a gentleman. He treats the performer with respect, and he is polite and considerate towards the lady artiste. This is especially the case in the Spanish-speaking countries.

We made a second tour of Switzerland in the winter. At Christmas we were at the beautiful town of Lausanne, where Gamboli arranged a series of living statuary groups appropriate to the season. In one of these poses I represented Abel, and Mr Gamboli was an angel bearing me to Heaven after being murdered by Cain. I suppose that scriptural subjects for living statues would not be approved of by English audiences; but in Switzerland they were received with enthusiastic applause. In the tableau of Abraham and Isaac, little Henry, Lily Gamboli's boy, appeared as Isaac, and he also posed in other Biblical scenes.

From Switzerland we went to the South of France, and here our good luck changed. We visited the lovely town of Nice, and went on to Marseilles; but business was far from brisk. At Monte Carlo we were more successful; and I had my first peep at the gambling tables, though I had no money to gamble with.

While at the old town of Perpignan, one of the most picturesque places in Europe, Lily and I were greatly terrified by hearing that a prowling gang of robbers were committing violent assaults upon women after dark, and robbing them of their money and jewellery. They were quite reckless in their thefts, and if they could not unfasten a woman's earrings they would actually slice off a bit of her ear with a sharp knife.

You may be sure that Gamboli would not allow us to go out alone if he could help it. But now and then he was busy in the *café chantant* till late in the evening, and Lily and I used to walk home together. We chose the best-lighted streets, and often went a roundabout way to avoid dark and suspicious thoroughfares.

Fortunately, Gamboli became acquainted with the leader of this desperate gang, whom he met one day in a café. The robber appeared to like him, for his manners were always polite and amiable, and the two conversed together for a while. Upon parting, the leader of the robbers said to Gamboli; "Well, monsieur, I know that the ladies of your company sometimes go home unattended in the dark. But do not fear; I will see to it that they are not molested."

After this comforting assurance Lily and I were not afraid to be out after nightfall.

From Perpignan we worked our way by the magnificent Pyrenees Mountains to the border of Spain, by way of Port Bou. At this place we were hard up for the first time since leaving England. The prospect seemed desperate. We had not enough money for our railway fares into Spain, and there was very little hope of obtaining food and lodging on credit. In my next chapter I will tell how we contrived to escape from this plight, thanks to Mr Gamboli's cleverness.

CHAPTER V

MY SPANISH ADMIRER

LILY and I were in great anxiety. My friend was in a more serious predicament, for she had a child, whom she loved with intense devotion. It is bad enough to be stranded and penniless in an English town; but the situation is far worse when an artiste is far from home and in a strange land. However, it was useless to sit down and cry over our misfortunes; something had to be done at once.

Leaving us in a café, Gamboli went out and explored the town. He was away for some time, and we began to wonder what had happened. We were too distressed to talk, and we were both hungry. At last he returned, and we saw from the expression on his face that he had not been entirely unsuccessful.

"We can show to-night in the casino," he said cheerfully. "But I'm in a fix about a pianist; there is no one to play the accompaniments to the dances."

What was to be done? We were delighted with this chance of earning a pound or so, but it looked as though the chance would be lost for the want of a pianist. We could not dance without music.

Gamboli lit a cigarette and sat down to think. We could see no way out of the difficulty. Poor little Henry began to complain of hunger, and we tried to comfort him as best we could.

Suddenly from the distance came the sound of a piano organ in the street. Gamboli jumped up.

"I've got it," he cried. "We'll engage the piano organ. We'll have our orchestra after all." And he ran out of the café and up the street.

A DANCING GIRL

The organ grinder was a Frenchman. He listened to Gamboli's proposal, and fell in with it, arranging to play for us for a share of our evening's takings. We rejoiced to think that there was at last a way out of our difficulty.

The casino where we performed was a small one. There was a little stage, and the hall was furnished with tables and chairs. It was the chief place of entertainment in the town.

About seven o'clock we were dressed and ready for our performance. Lily and I were in our dancing-skirts, tights, and pumps. We had rehearsed two or three dances to the organ accompaniment, and one of them was a cake-walk. I shall never forget dancing an American cake-walk to a French waltz air. It was a quaint performance, but the audience were delighted, and we gained an encore.

We performed for four nights in this little town, and when we left we had about enough money to pay our fares to Gerona. This is a very quaint town, with a most beautiful cathedral and some ancient churches. There is a café in the town that is well patronized in the evenings, when a sort of variety entertainment is given. Here we pleased the audience with our statuary groups and dancing.

Lily and I had learned the tambourine dance, which went very well in Spain, and I performed the favourite sailor's hornpipe.

Spain is a delightful country, and the people are charming. The scenery is glorious, and the sun seems always to be shining its brightest.

In a few weeks I began to pick up a little Spanish. I knew a smattering of French and German, but I was quite unacquainted with the language of Spain when I entered the country. But when one is travelling it is necessary to speak the language, and I soon knew enough to get on with in the shops and restaurants.

At Barcelona we stayed for five months, and I look back on that time as one of the happiest in my life. Barcelona is the busiest and perhaps the wealthiest city in Spain, and it is well provided with places of amusement. There are several variety halls, and I have performed in all of them.

For our living statuary show we represented the figures of various public statues in the streets, and these groups were very popular in every large town of Spain. The idea was Mr Gamboli's, and it was a decided success. We studied the statues very carefully, and reproduced them as truthfully as possible.

In Barcelona I was taken for a Spaniard. I am very dark, and as I wore a mantilla and a black dress, I passed as a Spanish artiste. But I am afraid that when I tried to speak the language of the country my foreign accent was evident.

It was at Barcelona that we offended a *café chantant* audience. For the first time in my experience our dancing was greeted with hissing and hooting almost as soon as Lily and I came on to the stage. We were quite astounded. The whole house rose, and the din was tremendous. The orchestra stopped playing, and the manager, who came into the wings, beckoned us off the stage. We obeyed him, wondering what we had done to annoy the audience.

"Ladies," he explained, "I much regret that the people are angry; but the fact is, in Spain we do not think it decent for women to appear on the stage in such short skirts as you are wearing. Such a costume will never be tolerated."

Lily and I looked at one another in extreme astonishment. The skirts we were wearing were longer and much more decorous than the short, gauzy skirts worn by the ballet dancers in England. We had appeared in these costumes in France and Switzerland, and not a single member of the audience had ever objected. It was strange that the Spaniards should disapprove. However, every country has its own customs, and apparently the short skirt is forbidden on the stage in Barcelona.

As the audience protested so vehemently against our attire, we never appeared again in the offending dancing-skirts.

This was the only difficulty that we encountered with the audiences in Barcelona. In all the halls, including the one where we were hissed, we became one of the most popular "turns" on the programme.

I was very interested in the Spanish dancing, which I often saw in the variety halls of Barcelona, and I began to practise the Bolero, the Jota, and other dances. In a month or so I was able to perform the national dances in public, and, as I stated before, I was often taken for a Spanish dancer.

Much has been written upon the gallantry of Spanish men. They are certainly skilful in paying compliments to women, and they are very ardent lovers. When walking in the street, women of the middle and the upper classes are usually attended by a duenna or chaperon; but this rule is not always observed. A woman who goes out alone is certain to be addressed by men. I do not say that the remarks passed are not of a seemly kind. The Spanish majo, or "masher," has quite a store of compliments which he pays to any pretty woman who takes his fancy.

At first I used to be surprised and amused as a man murmured when I passed him: " Your eyes are brighter than the stars," or " The flowers bow when they see you coming "; but I became accustomed to this sort of flattery, and I soon learnt that it is empty enough, and often meant as chaff.

Occasionally presents and letters were left for me at the stage door. Some of the gifts were gloves, silk scarves, and boxes of chocolates. As for the missives, they were often written in a very high-flown language, and were mostly the effusions of young boys who had seen me on the stage.

I do not wish to appear egotistical and vain; I merely relate what befalls most girls in my profession, especially in Spain, where the artistes are very popular among the public. Before I left Barcelona I received a letter of a more serious kind, in which the writer declared the profoundest affection for me.

The letter that was handed to me by the manager was addressed in an elegant handwriting, which I did not recognize. I took it into the dressing-room, and sat down on my wardrobe basket. When I

A DANCING GIRL

glanced at the first page of the letter I saw that it was full of very ardent protestations of love. The writer was a Spaniard; but he had a little knowledge of English, and he had been at great pains to write a poetical and high-flown epistle. I was compared to the rose and the orange blossom; I was described as "divine," "exquisitely beautiful," and so on.

I could only smile at the fervour of the writer, who was a total stranger to me. He signed himself José, but he gave no address. I was, however, implored to "allow him the honour of speaking to me" upon leaving the hall on the following night.

Naturally, the letter aroused my curiosity. We all like flattery and compliments, and this admirer certainly excelled all others in the art of writing sentimental letters. It was the most fervid letter I had ever received.

I tried to imagine what this José was like. Was he young or old, tall or short, dark or fair? Was he rich or poor, handsome or plain? The letter gave me no answer to these questions. But somehow it seemed to me that the writer was middle-aged.

I cannot say that the letter caused me a sleepless night, or that it affected my appetite the next morning. Still, I will frankly confess that I felt very curious about my unknown correspondent. My curiosity deepened towards evening. When I went on the stage I wondered if he was among the audience. Could that bald-headed man in the front seats be he?

I changed my dress as quickly as possible after our turn, and then went into the street. The night was dark and breezeless, for it was August, and the day had been intensely hot. No one was in sight as I stepped into the street. Where was my admirer? I walked along feeling somewhat disappointed. Then suddenly I heard a voice behind me: " Señorita, señorita, I implore you!"

I turned round and saw a young fellow about sixteen. He was dark, with a very faint black moustache, and he wore the usual sombrero or Spanish hat, which he raised with an elegant sweep of his arm.

Curiosity impelled me to listen to him. I permitted him to walk with me under the palm trees of a quiet square.

Unfortunately Señor José was unable to converse much in English, though he could write my language fairly well. He made the most valiant efforts to please me; but most of his words were pronounced so curiously that I could not understand them. I have no doubt that the boy really fancied himself in love, for his tone was most ardent, and he vowed that he was ready to do anything that I commanded. I was not, however, able to reciprocate his love on the spot. He was a complete stranger to me, and though he was handsome I did not feel attracted to him.

If I gave José any hope, it was only because he appeared in a desperate state and talked of suicide. For weeks he shadowed me. He insisted on sending me presents of tea, which is a luxury in Spain. Hearing that most English women liked tea, he showered pounds of it upon me, although I protested frequently.

But though this episode was at first

rather amusing, it became tragic before long. I hope I was not heartless; I did not intend to be so; but José persisted in meeting me after I had told him plainly that I was not in love with him.

It was with José that I saw my first and last bull-fight. José was an enthusiastic lover of the national recreation, and the bull-fighting was one of his favourite subjects of conversation. I always protested that the sport was very cruel to the poor horses that are gored to death by the bull; but José could not understand such squeamishness. He argued that the horses were old, and only fit to be killed. And, after all, what was the death of four or five horses when the amusement gave such delight to thousands of spectators?

After much persuasion, I consented to attend a great bull-fight which was to be held on a feast day. José met me an hour before the show. He was dressed foppishly and wore his sombrero a little tilted, while he smoked a big cigar. He insisted on buying me a fan, saying that every lady at a bull-fight used a fan. So, with my mantilla and fan, and looking for all the

A DANCING GIRL

world like a Spanish doña, I went with José to the Plaza de Toros.

The seats were thronged with people of all classes, the fashionable set occupying the seats in the shade. It was a glorious day, and the scene was most interesting, the seats being packed with Barcelona folk in their holiday attire. A splendid orchestra played selections from Italian operas and some inspiriting marches while the place was filling with spectators. Then the picadors on their horses rode into the ring, followed by the men who throw the little darts, and four famous toreros, or swordsmen, who face the infuriated bull singly after he has been irritated and maddened by the picadors and the dart-throwers.

It was a fine sight, for the costumes were most picturesque and gorgeous. I was beginning to enjoy the spectacle of the grand entry, the fine music of the band, and the sight of the gaily-attired spectators, when the ring was cleared, a door thrown open, and a big black bull rushed into the ring. The men on horseback trotted in, and began to worry the beast with their lances. Three times he charged, and one of the horsemen received him on the point of the weapon. Then the bull drew back, and stood snorting for a moment or two before a charge. At the next rush one of his sharp horns entered the side of a wretched bony horse. It was the first blood. I covered my face with my hands, and I heard the people shouting excitedly.

"The horse is dying," said José, " and the picador fell to the ground. Ah! that is a splendid bull. Why do you not look, Señorita Marion?"

Well, curiosity forced me to look again upon the blood-stained ring, and I saw the swordsman, called the espada, standing motionless in front of the bull. Both the animal and the man were as still as statues. It was a terrible moment. I was horrified, but I gazed on the scene. Slowly the bull advanced, lashing his flanks with his tail, and still the man stood facing him, gently fluttering a red cloth. Again and again I saw the bull charge and the espada step aside. It was a wonderful performance.

But the death scene quite upset my nerves. I saw the man plunge the sword, almost to the hilt, into the neck of the bull. I had seen enough of this bloodshed and cruelty. A sickness came over me; I felt that I could not look at the ring again.

"I must go out; I've seen enough," I said to my companion.

"Oh, you have seen nothing yet," he said. "There are five more bulls to be killed this afternoon. We shall see some fine play, I tell you."

"No, no; I have seen too much," I said. "I am quite sickened; I must go out."

I am afraid that José was seriously annoyed with me, for he would insist on coming out of the building.

"Don't disturb yourself," I said. "I am an English girl, and we know how to look after ourselves. I will go straight to my lodgings, so don't trouble to come."

But José would not hear of my going home alone. He said that no gentleman in Spain would permit a lady friend to leave him in this manner.

"No, I will certainly accompany you," he said firmly.

It was on our way home from the bull-fight that we passed a dark, pale-faced girl, with a piercing glance, who looked closely at me, and halted as though she would speak. I noticed that José turned his head away, and that he appeared agitated. But I did not ask him any questions, nor did I attach any importance to the incident. I was rather puzzled, however, by José's silence as we walked along. I thought that he was vexed at losing a greater part of the afternoon's entertainment in the Plaza de Toros.

When we came to the door of the house where I was staying with the Gambolis, Don José raised his hat in his usual gallant fashion, and paid me a parting compliment.

For three days I saw nothing of José. I began to wonder if he had got over the infatuation and found another object for his affection. On the evening of the third day I saw the black-eyed, pale girl in the front seats when I came on the stage. I

A DANCING GIRL

recognized her at once. Her eyes were fixed upon me, and they had an expression of hate and anger that I shall never forget.

Upon the next night she was there again. She curled her lip when I came on the stage, and, as before, fastened her black eyes upon me. When I went to the wings her angry look followed me in a menacing manner.

While I was changing my clothes the thought flashed upon me that this girl was bent on annoying me. It was already my suspicion that she was in love with José. Jealousy was preying upon her, and no doubt she meant mischief.

"I believe she is waiting for me in the street at this moment," I said to myself as I put on my mantilla.

The hall was in a quarter of narrow alleys, and they were not well lighted. I came out, and walked along the street in the direction of my lodgings. At the third turning I saw a woman standing in a doorway. As I drew near I recognized my supposed rival.

A word with you, Englishwoman," said

the girl, flashing her eyes upon me, and speaking between her teeth.

"What do you want?" I said.

"You have robbed me of the love of José Torso," she cried vehemently.

"No, you are mistaken. I do not love him; I am merely his friend——"

She would not allow me to finish. I had observed that her right hand was held behind her. Suddenly she brought her hand in front of her, and I saw the flash of steel. She grasped a navaja, a long Spanish knife. There was no one in sight. I do not pretend that I was not alarmed, for there was murder in her eyes.

"Thank Heaven I am strong and a gymnast!" was the thought that darted into my mind.

The girl with the knife drew back a step and lowered the blade. I knew that in Spain the dagger was used with an upward thrust, the object being to tear the flesh of an opponent. Had I moved, she would have plunged the knife into my back. I stood glaring into her eyes. It seemed minutes, but it was only brief seconds. With a leap, she advanced. I stepped aside and grasped her right shoulder, and we struggled. A sharp pain shot in my left arm, but I held my assailant and secured both her wrists.

With all my strength I twisted her arm. I saw her wince with pain. We struggled up and down the side walk. Presently, to my surprise, she gave a cry and implored me to loose her wrists. I did so, and the knife fell on the ground. In a couple of seconds she was round the corner.

Then I realized why she had suddenly flown. A civil guard was pacing slowly towards me. I thrust the dagger out of sight within my bodice, hoping that he had not seen the struggle, for I dreaded a police case.

Fortunately, the officer had not noticed us grappling. The street was ill-lighted, and we were in the shadow of a tall building. I returned his good-night, and hurried away, feeling glad when I reached a wide, brightly-lighted thoroughfare.

My heart was beating at an alarming pace. I had narrowly escaped a horrible wound, if not death itself. As it was, my left arm was cut, and the blood soaked through my sleeve.

I reached home quite nerve-shaken. The wound on my arm was not serious, and I washed it carefully and bound it up with a couple of handkerchiefs.

The dagger that I had captured was a terrible weapon; the blade was over a foot long, and very pointed and keen, and the handle was of horn inlaid with brass. I put it in a drawer among other mementoes of Spain, such as photographs, ribbons, a couple of painted fans, and a Manila shawl.

I sank into a chair and began to take myself to task for allowing Don José to pay me attentions. Yet, after all, I had told him from the beginning that I did not love him. Was I to blame? Anyway, I felt very much upset by this affair. I had unwittingly aroused a murderous jealousy in another woman.

All night I lay awake thinking of this black-haired, pale girl, and the ferocious gleam of her eyes when she flourished the navaja before me. I was afraid that I might have a fearful nightmare if I slept. For several nights after this adventure I was troubled with dreams in which José and the girl figured.

What had become of José? He had not been to the hall for eight days. Was he also in fear of the girl's wild jealousy? I did not know where he lived, for he had always kept this a secret. I soon learnt why he had not divulged his private affairs beyond telling me that he had plenty of money and was the son of an important man in Barcelona.

One day I went into a draper's shop in the Calle de Fernando Septimo. A young man in a dim corner came forward to serve me. It was José. I shall never forget his embarrassment. He stammered and stuttered for two or three minutes, and I could hardly keep from laughing.

"Ah," he said, "you will be astonished, no doubt. I am, indeed, as I told you, the son of a grandee; but suddenly we have lost all our wealth, and for three days I have been in this business. I have meant to write to you and to explain all."

Poor José. He coloured up to his

eyebrows and looked extremely ridiculous. I was really sorry for him. No doubt he had been through much trouble with the girl who tried to stab me. He was so terribly nervous and ashamed that I soon hurried from the shop.

Once again I saw José. One Sunday, while strolling on the beautiful Rambla under the palm trees, I saw him with the black-haired girl seated at a table outside a café. They were drinking syrup and water, and seemed quite happy.

CHAPTER VI

ADVENTURES IN SPAIN

OUR five months at Barcelona were drawing to an end. The time had flown, for we had been busy and happy. No money affairs had cast a cloud over our days or caused us restless, anxious nights. But it was time to move on. We had worked all the variety halls and cafés of

A DANCING GIRL

importance, and we had no novel "numbers." Gamboli thought we ought to go to the Balearic Islands and try our fortune at Palma, the chief town.

These lovely islands in the Mediterranean Sea are four in number, and the largest is Majorca, or Mallorca, as the Spaniards call it. They are not much visited yet by tourists, but they will, no doubt, become favourite holiday resorts in the future. The scenery is delightful, both inland and along the coast, and at present the living is very cheap.

Steamboats travel regularly to Palma from Barcelona, and we took tickets for the voyage. The passage proved very adventurous and alarming. Before we started, the weather had been sultry and intensely hot. Even the nights were breathless and close. I suppose it was the calm that precedes a storm, for no sooner had we left Barcelona than a wind arose, and in half an hour it was blowing a perfect hurricane.

Mr Gamboli learned from the captain of the vessel that the storm was likely to become more violent as we approached the islands. Poor little Henry was quite terrified; and I must confess that when I saw the seething expanse of water, and heard the terrifying roar of the wind and the waves, I felt anxious for our safety.

I was not troubled with sea-sickness, so I could remain on deck and watch the wild scene of angry water. However, the captain soon ordered us below, saying that he could not be responsible for any passenger that stayed on deck. So we were cooped up in a little cabin and left to the mercy of the weather.

I have never passed through a worse storm at sea. The ship was tossed about like a mere cockle-shell, and the waves poured continually across the deck and down into the cabin. Passengers rolled out of their bunks, and china fell now and again with a crash. The din was tremendous. Sometimes the ship stood still, though the engines were panting vigorously. Then the vessel rose on the top of a huge surging wave, and went down headlong into the trough.

Some of us sat pale and silent. I doubted whether we would ever see

Palma. I saw old and young folk paralysed with fear. In one corner a priest knelt, praying for help; and two lovers sat hand in hand, resolved to die together. When the storm was at the height of its fury some one declared that the captain had expressed the dread that the ship would go down presently.

"My friends," said the priest in a loud, solemn tone, "we are in fearful danger. Nothing is left but the mercy of God."

As the priest spoke, a wave, larger than any that had struck the vessel, swept across the deck and carried away some of the gear. The engine was thudding with all steam on, but we were not able to make any way against the hurricane. We heard the captain shout to the crew, but his voice was drowned in the tremendous howling of the wind and the noise of the white-capped waves.

A great fear was upon us as we huddled in the cabin. It was awful to be imprisoned in this way, while we feared that the ship might capsize at any moment. I felt that I would rather be on deck, in spite of the danger.

I suppose that the storm was too violent to last long. We had passed through the worst of the rough water, and soon we were told that the danger was almost over. We all breathed again freely, and the priest returned thanks to Providence for delivering us from the cruelty of the waves. Beyond some damage to the boat there was no other mishap.

We reached the port several hours late, and found a large crowd on the quay. The people had feared the worst. You may be sure that we were all glad to step on to firm land. Some of the passengers were prostrated by sea-sickness, and all had endured terror during our wild crossing.

Palma impressed me as a delightful and picturesque town. We found quarters in a little fonda, or inn, near the sea. In two days we had an offer to give our show at the principal place of entertainment. It was a hall chiefly patronized by men, who were mostly dressed in the quaint costume of the island.

The people did not, at the first glance,

appear to be very strait-laced or proper; but we soon learned that they were extremely decorous in one respect. Quite forgetting our experiences at Barcelona, we appeared on the stage in our ordinary dancing-skirts. There was at first a dead silence. Then, as we began to dance, a murmur ran through the crowd, which rose to a roar. Hisses, yells, and hootings were directed upon us. We continued to dance, hoping that the din would cease presently; but the noise only increased, and some of the audience stood up in a threatening manner.

The manager, who seemed much alarmed, called us off the stage. He was very indignant. Gamboli tried to pacify him, but he threw his arms about, and declared that we had ruined his reputation. It was useless to argue with the man.

"I cannot pay you full salary; it is impossible!" he cried.

"But the ladies will wear longer dresses!" exclaimed Gamboli.

"They must certainly do so. At the same time, this affair has done me harm with the public, and I shall lose money through it. I can't pay you the price agreed upon."

After much discussion the manager decided that we must either accept £5 less on a week's salary or not perform at all. As we needed the money, and saw no alternative, we had to accept these reduced terms during the time that we remained in the island.

It may surprise some English readers that the Spanish people are so prudish in this matter. They are certainly not squeamish in many things, but they will not tolerate short dancing-skirts. In England, as I have said, such a costume does not arouse comment.

After our visit to Palma we returned to the mainland, and had a beautifully calm passage. We spent one night in Barcelona, and went on to Tarragona, a town of about thirty thousand inhabitants. There are two theatres here and some singing cafés, and we soon found an engagement.

The place was not very prosperous, but the people seemed to have plenty of time to enjoy themselves. I liked Tarragona very much, and I was never tired of sitting on the promenade of Santa Clara, watching the blue waters of the Mediterranean Sea.

The weather was tropical. We found our dancing very exhausting in this excessive heat. While at Tarragona we almost lived on green figs, which were in season and very plentiful. In such a hot climate one does not relish meat dishes, and it was a pleasant change to live as vegetarians.

From Tarragona we travelled to Madrid —a long journey in the heat. The capital of Spain is perhaps the most modern town in the country, and it reminded me somewhat of Paris and Brussels. It is well paved and lighted, and there are electric tramways and other modern improvements. The royal palace is here, and the city has a large number of wealthy and fashionable residents, who live for amusement.

Our biggest success in Madrid was with a representation in living statuary of the famous monument of the Dós de Mayo, or Second of May. This monument is in memory of the soldiers who fought against the French rulers in the time of Murat, and it has beautiful figures in groups around a granite sarcophagus. We selected various groups of the statuary, and presented them one evening to an enthusiastic audience.

The Dos de Mayo groups were a huge success. Managers competed with one another in offers, and we had no lack of engagements while the novelty of the show lasted. We made a round of the popular variety halls and some of the larger cafés, and had a busy time.

A number of English variety performers visit Madrid, and one of the halls is managed by an Englishman. I was glad to meet some of my own countrymen, and to hear my own language spoken again. We sometimes met in one of the cafés to talk "shop." I had been away from England so long that it seemed ages since I started out with the Primrose Girls on the fateful tour. From the English artistes I heard the latest professional gossip.

In Madrid I made the acquaintance of a lion-tamer at one of the halls. He was a handsome, daring man, and very successful in his business. His lions were said to be the fiercest on the road, and they were certainly the most ferocious I have ever seen.

As I have already said, lions fed on cooked meat are tamer than those fed upon raw flesh. I know an American tamer who can do anything with his lions, and he never allows them to taste uncooked food. But the performer in Madrid always gave his lions raw meat, to keep them fierce. He also took other measures to make them savage.

One day I was in the hall an hour before the show, talking to the lion king. Presently he calmly lit a cigarette, and, taking a heavy whip, with a thick lash and a weighted handle, he entered the cage. Immediately the lions drew into a corner and began to snarl and to show their huge teeth. Rating them at the top of his voice, the tamer began to lay about with the whip, till the lions were leaping about the cage. His well-directed cuts fell upon their heads and flanks, and he beat them severely.

I could not bear the sight. I have a

love for animals, and it seemed to me that this flogging was quite unnecessary. He was not correcting the animals, but merely irritating them. I turned away from the cage.

"Ah," shouted the trainer, " you don't like to see them whipped. Let me tell you, señorita, I must master them, or they would quickly master me." And he continued to lash the beasts with vigour. I shall not be surprised if this lion king loses his life one of these days, for he is intensely hated by his lions.

Madrid is a gay city, and people of all nations may be seen in the places of amusement. The chief theatres are the Royal, the Princess's, and the Comedy; and the popular houses are the España, the Lara, the Apollo, the Zarzuela, and the Eslava. Short shows of about an hour are given in some of the smaller theatres and variety halls, in which sketches and one-act plays are acted, followed by various turns, such as dancing and acrobatics. In the summer a theatre is opened in the chief public park.

My experience of the Spanish variety

performances is that they are, on the whole, more artistic than those of England and America, and freer from vulgarity. The variety artiste in Spain works hard at his business, and takes a pride in it, and in return the public are grateful to him for amusing them, and do not look upon him as an idler.

The fact is, the people of Spain are all more or less artists at heart, and they will not tolerate a poor performance, whether it is that of an actor or of a dancer. They appreciate good work, and expect it, and they are prepared to pay the artiste well. In dress, music, dancing, and many other ways, the Spanish show their natural taste for art.

I was not a little proud that I could please Madrid audiences with my dancing, for Spain is the home of the dance, and even little children are critics of the art. It pleased the Spanish folk that I could use the castanets like one of their own countrywomen, and perform the national dances. But they were perhaps more pleased with the " danse Inglés," the sailor's hornpipe, which they always applauded heartily.

While I was at Madrid I made friends with a charming Spanish girl of eighteen named Dolores. She was the daughter of a violinist who had become paralysed and unable to follow his occupation. His wife had been dead two years, and the son was in the army. Poor señor was very patient, in spite of his terrible malady and the poverty that it had brought to the home. He lived with his daughter Dolores in one room in a small street near the church of San Isidro, where I often visited them. They were a devoted pair, and Dolores was the support of her father in his infirmity, working early and late as a dressmaker in a business of her own.

Dolores was a typical Spanish beauty. Her face was oval and refined, the skin a light olive, slightly tinged with pink on the cheeks, and her eyes were dark, tender, and lustrous, with a look of thoughtful sadness in them. She was one of the loveliest girls I have ever met, and very gentle in disposition.

Among her customers was an Englishwoman, a Miss Ray, whose brother was connected with the iron export trade at Bilbao. Mr Ray was often at Madrid on business, when he stayed with his sister in the Calle de Alcalá. One day George Ray saw Dolores at his sister's boarding-house. He fell in love with her at first sight, and, learning her story, he came to see her father. Mr Ray was very sympathetic, and he wished to do something for the old man. At the same time, he was deeply in love with Dolores.

At the end of a week Dolores came to me at the hall one night to seek my advice. She said that Mr Ray had offered to marry her, and that she loved him.

"He is so kind and so handsome," she said with a sigh.

"Why do you sigh, Dolores?" I asked. "It ought to make you happy."

"Ah, my friend, I sigh because I can't leave my poor father. He has been good to me, and he loves me, and I must be a good daughter to him."

"It is hard for you, Dolores," I said, kissing her.

"Mr Ray wishes me to leave Spain.

He is going to South America, to the Argentine, and he wants me to marry at once and to go with him. But I cannot leave my father. Oh, what can I do?"

I was very touched by my friend's perplexity. Think as I would, I felt that I could not advise her in this difficult matter. I tried to think of a plan, but the situation seemed hopeless. If she would not leave her father, nothing could be done.

Mr Ray continued to press Dolores to go with him. He offered to pay some one to keep house for the señor; but Dolores would not hear of this, for she thought that no one in the world could take care of her father save herself. I think I was the only person who knew how Dolores suffered, for she kept her trouble from her father. She was very noble. At the same time, she was sacrificed, as so many women are, to an idea of duty.

Mr Ray left Madrid, greatly disappointed that Dolores would not accompany him. My friend was broken-hearted. I tried to console her, but she became very depressed, and her health was affected.

Mr Ray wrote one letter to Dolores from Argentina; then he went out of her life as suddenly as he had come into it. She never heard of him again, and Miss Ray, his sister, soon left Madrid for Scotland.

This trouble preyed for long on Dolores' mind. I am afraid that she will never quite recover from it. Spanish women are capable of remarkably strong affection, and they do not hide their feelings like their English sisters. I was struck with the difference between the Spanish and English women in this respect, and in many others. The women of Spain are more feminine than English women. They are splendid wives and affectionate mothers, and if they are backward in education, they have still much character and intelligence. It is not true that the Spanish women are treacherous and disloyal, and that they carry a dagger thrust into their garters. There are many mistakes made by foreigners about the people of Spain. I can only say that I found them delightful. They are honest in their dealings, very loyal to friends, and free from artificiality. Their courtesy is not a thing of pretence, but based on kindness of heart and consideration for others.

So devoted are the Spanish to their families, that they hate to be separated from relatives. Family affection keeps many Spaniards from roaming, and in this matter they are unlike the British or the Germans. The Spanish dancers and artistes who visit England rarely come without bringing several relatives with them. An artiste will stipulate that his mother and sisters shall accompany him before he will sign an agent's contract. It is said in the profession in England that if you engage one Spanish artiste you engage a company.

Affection and sentiment count more to the Spaniard than making money. This is to me one of the attractive qualities of the Spanish race.

While I was still concerned about Dolores I met another girl in trouble. She was English, and had been on the variety stage as a singer and dancer. At Nottingham she met an illusionist who was performing at the same music-hall, and this artiste exercised a great fascination over Rose Nevill. To be plain, Rose had thrown in her lot with this man and had come to Spain with him.

I first met Rose Nevill at a café which was the resort of actors and variety artistes. She was seated alone reading a letter, and there were tears in her eyes. Her face was pale and anxious, and she seemed in deep grief. I did not wish to pry into her private affairs, but it was evident that she was in trouble; and by her dress and appearance I recognized that she was one of my countrywomen. Presently our eyes met, and she smiled faintly. I felt impelled to speak to her. She told me the strange tale of her career, which I must relate in my next chapter.

CHAPTER VII

THE STUDENT OF COIMBRA

"YOU are, like me, an English artiste," said the girl as I sat down by her side. "I have seen you on the stage. I am in trouble," she added, after a short pause.

"Perhaps I can help you," I returned.

"I'm afraid you can't," she said, shaking her head. "It is not a matter in which anyone can help me. But I am quite alone in Madrid, and I would like to tell you of my trouble."

I ordered some coffee, and Rose began her story in a low tone.

"My father was a commercial traveller, and we lived in Sheffield. I was one of three girls, and we were all put to business. I was apprenticed to the drapery, and I served my time. I never liked the business; it was quite uninteresting to me, and I was a failure in it. My heart was set pon going on the stage, and I longed to be a comedy actress. Soon after the end of my apprenticeship to Messrs B—— and Co. I asked my father to allow me to go on the stage. He was a very religious man, with a horror of the theatre, and he sternly forbade me from becoming an actress.

"Well, the passion for the stage was strong upon me, and, to make a long story short, I saved a pound or two and borrowed some more money, and went up to London to see agents. I can't say how many I called upon, but at last I obtained an engagement to 'walk on' in a musical comedy at a pound a week. I had no lines and no part; I was just one of a crowd. However, it was a beginning, and I managed to live on a pound a week in one small room.

"I told my parents what I was doing. My father cut me off; he refused to have anything to do with me unless I left the stage. But my mother wrote regularly to me.

"When the run of the piece was at an end I was out of work. I had just two pounds in the world, which I had saved at the expense of my appetite, for I lived very plainly indeed. One of the girls who walked on with me had been on the halls for a time, and she said that if we went into partnership we might do well as duettists and dancers. She offered to teach me the business. I liked this girl, and I was glad to do anything to keep starvation at bay.

"I needn't tell you much about my partnership with Joan. We led an up-and-down life for about a year, singing in small halls and with touring variety combinations. Our top salary was six pounds a week, and our usual pay came to about thirty shillings each. As we were 'out of a shop' for five months in the year, you can guess how hard-driven we were.

"One day Joan said that she was going to marry a sketch artiste who was just starting for South Africa. It was a shock to me. I had to look about now for a job on my own.

"I began the usual tour of the London agents. In a few days I was 'on the rocks'

A DANCING GIRL

I remember starting out without any breakfast to call on an agent on the Surrey side. I had been told that this man was booking girls for pantomime, and that there was a good chance of an engagement for the provinces in a fit-up company.

"The agent was a middle-aged man, very coarse to look at, and quite as coarse in his language. One does not object to the familiarity of agents if they don't go too far, as their chaff means nothing. But this fellow was a perfect brute. He very soon made suggestions to me which I leave to your imagination. Now, up to lately I've kept quite straight, and when this man made advances I grew highly indignant. He simply laughed at me.

"'If you're so jolly particular, you'd better chuck this business,' he said with a leer.

"After enduring his coarseness for some time, hoping that he would talk business, I left the office, feeling that I had been horribly insulted.

"I tell you this because I was then leading a respectable life, and because I want you to understand that I got into trouble through mistaken affection.

"And now," said Rose, with a choke in her voice, "I must tell you that I met a young man in the profession who made violent love to me, and promised to be true for life. I won't deny that I knew what I was doing. But I was in love with this man. We could not marry, for his wife is living, though he separated from her five years ago."

She stopped for a moment, overcome with grief. Then she continued:

"Well, we came to Madrid a fortnight ago, and now he has left me, and gone off to Paris with another woman. I am almost penniless, and I am deserted. I have just one peseta left."

It was a common story, but none the less sad. My heart ached for poor Rose. What could I do for her? I tried to think of a plan, and I pressed some money upon her.

For two days I spent a greater part of my leisure time in calling upon managers whom I knew, and trying to find work for Rose. But I was unsuccessful; there were no vacancies anywhere. Meanwhile I kept the girl going on what money I could spare.

One day an idea struck me. We had made the acquaintance of an artist who painted figure subjects. I had posed for him two or three times as a classical dancer in Grecian dress. I went to see Señor Casa, and asked him if he would engage Rose as a model.

The artist replied that he was glad to know of a model, but she must sit for the nude. He wanted a model for a Psyche figure, to be included in a group in a symbolic painting.

"Send your friend to me," said Señor Casa. "She may be just the girl I want."

I went to Rose's lodgings and told her of this chance. She was not so delighted as I expected her to be. At first her face brightened, but when she heard that she must stand undraped she recoiled from the idea. I argued that there was no disgrace whatever in being a model, and told her that this opportunity was not to be despised when she was in such difficulties.

Poor Rose! At last she overcame her scruples, and went to the studio. She trusted Señor Casa most confidently, for he was an honourable gentleman.

I saw Rose once only after she became a model. She said she was saving up enough money to pay her passage to England, and that in a few weeks she would leave Spain.

Rose Nevill was very soft-hearted and emotional, and a curious mixture of prudery and a love of pleasure. She was exceedingly squeamish about posing as Psyche, and yet she had no objection to appearing in tights. She liked wine when she could afford it, and she drank pretty freely. But she was horrified when she saw me light a Cuban cigarette. Many of the public think that all women in the variety profession are loose in their morals. Yet, as I have said before, I have met with curious prudery in my profession, and I can assure my readers that many women artistes are as strait-laced as Quakeresses.

From the capital of Spain we travelled to Oporto, the second largest town in

Portugal, where we opened at a popular variety theatre with our dancing and statuary show. Oporto is a splendid city on the banks of the River Douro. I have never seen anywhere such beautiful gardens as those of the Crystal Palace, which is built on a steep hill overhanging the river. The views from the winding paths of the Crystal Palace, looking down the Douro to the sea, are magnificent, especially at sunset.

There are many English people at Oporto, and there is much bustle in the streets. The shops are large, and in the English or Parisian style. Oporto is, in some respects, more modern than the large Spanish towns that I have visited.

I found the Portuguese people less attractive and picturesque than the Spaniards, but I have no fault to find with the way that artistes are treated by the managers and the audiences.

We were about a month in Oporto, and during our stay nothing of especial interest happened. But at Coimbra, our next town, we were to meet with an adventure of an exciting character.

Coimbra is even more beautiful than Oporto. It is a much smaller town, with less than 20,000 inhabitants; but it is prosperous, and the musical cafés are well patronized by the lively students of the university.

I shall have something to say presently of the ways of one of the students of Coimbra. They are a very gay set of young men, and they dress in a peculiar costume and play the guitar and mandoline.

The climate of Coimbra is so warm that dates ripen here, and oranges, lemons, and many other fruits are abundant.

The streets of Coimbra are extremely steep, and there is an upper and lower town. Above the higher town rises the university, which was once an old palace.

In this quaint and charming place we soon became popular with audiences. The students came night after night to the performance, and they always applauded our dancing with enthusiasm. We worked very hard to please them, and as the weather was extremely hot, I found dancing quite fatiguing, especially when encores were demanded by the noisy but appreciative students.

One night, after I had gone to bed, I heard voices in the street close to my window. My room was on the ground floor, and the window was open, as it was a stifling night. Presently a guitar was strummed lightly, and a man's tenor voice rang out. The words were in Portuguese, and I could not understand them, but the melody was sweet and plaintive.

I peeped under the curtain and saw a group of students. One played a guitar, and another sang the love ditty, while a third held a lantern on the end of a pole. I could only suppose that I was being serenaded by the party, and I felt flattered by this pretty attention.

I opened the window a few inches, and threw a rose into the street. The singer stooped, picked it up, and, after kissing it, put it in his buttonhole. Amused by his gallantry, I watched the group from behind the curtain. The guitar-player now struck up another air, and all the students joined in the chorus. It was quite romantic, and this serenading recalled what I had read about the old days in Spain and Portugal.

Presently a shower of gravel rattled on the window-panes. I lit the lamp, and, putting on a shawl, drew the curtain back. The handsome singer, with his hand on his heart, made a profound bow, and all the students raised their hats when I showed myself.

On the next day, as I was leaving the café after a rehearsal, I saw the tall, swarthy student advancing towards me. He raised his hat, and, in broken English, asked if he might speak a few words.

"We are so pleased with you and the other lady dancer that we desire to give you a benefit," he said.

"That is very kind," I answered.

"Ah, my charming English mees, it is a joy and a privilege to me," he said, bowing profoundly.

Well, I had better confess that I was attracted to this handsome student with the sweet tenor voice. His manners were delightful, and he knew how to pay the most charming compliments.

We had several walks together in the lovely Botanic Gardens and by the banks of the River Mondego. My companion certainly seemed to be sincere and honest. He was apparently very anxious that the benefit performance should be a great success.

"I will sell at least a hundred tickets for you," he said, over and over again.

Naturally, we all wished to profit by the kindness of the students of Coimbra; so Gamboli had a number of tickets printed for the benefit entertainment, and special bills were pasted up in the town. My attentive cavalier took fifty or sixty tickets, which he said he could sell without trouble.

For the benefit we rehearsed two new dances, and we arranged a very full bill. The café was partly filled when the curtain went up. When I came on the stage with Lily Gamboli to dance a duet I could not see my cavalier. Why was he not present? He usually sat in the front seats and applauded vigorously. I was puzzled at not seeing him in his usual place.

Between the turns Gamboli teased me a little.

"Where is your gallant admirer to-night?" he asked, with a laugh.

"I can't understand it," I said, feeling rather vexed with Dom Carlos.

But something of a far more disturbing nature occurred that night. I have spoken of the great heat in Coimbra, and that may explain what followed. Towards the end of the performance, just as I was going on the stage, a terrible rumbling sound was heard.

"Is that thunder?" I asked, turning to Gamboli.

Then I noticed that the stage was heaving. Something fell with a loud crash, and startled cries came from all parts of the house.

"It is an earthquake!" cried the manager. "Fly for your lives!"

Strange to say, my first thought was for my dress-basket and costumes. I turned to run to the dressing-room. As I fled along the passage the floor rocked and heaved like the deck of a vessel in a storm.

When I reached the dressing-room I saw the looking-glass sliding from the table, and the floor heaving in an alarming manner. With a crash, the glass fell to the floor, broken into fragments. A terror seized me, and I felt myself trembling. I flung my costumes out of the dressing-basket on to the floor, and grasped the most expensive of them and some of my stage jewellery, and turned to fly.

From all parts of the building there came cries of fear and distress. The manager came running along the passage, carrying a cash-box and some account-books.

"Fly, señora, fly!" he cried. "The roof will fall presently!"

I rushed to the front of the house, and found myself merged in a mass of struggling and shouting people. Every one was in a panic. Women screamed, and men struggled to escape from the jumble of terrified humanity that blocked the doorway. I kept my elbows stiff, and fought with the rest of the crowd, for it was no use to do otherwise. The panic-stricken crowd had lost all reason. My skirt was torn, and my hair disordered. Panting, crushed, and almost fainting, I was carried along with the seething mass into the street.

I staggered to a shop front and propped myself up to regain breath. But I was at last out of the building, and I was thankful. The whole town seemed crazy with fear. Women carrying children rushed down the streets without knowing where they were going. Tradesmen were throwing their goods into the roadway with frantic energy. It was a terrible scene. The whole world seemed toppling to destruction.

I can't say how long the tremors lasted, but it seemed many minutes after I reached the street before the shock was over. The road was strewn with the shopkeepers' things, and the people were kneeling down praying to God and the Holy Virgin for help. I was fearfully anxious concerning my friend Lily, her child, and her husband, for I could not see them anywhere.

As soon as I recovered breath, I hastened to the little hotel where we were staying. To my great joy, I found my friends there, safely seated in the dining-room They were pale and excited, and little Henry was crying with fear.

" Thank God we're saved! " said Gamboli reverently.

The shock had been very severe. Several buildings in the town were damaged, and the people were half mad with terror. A wind had sprung up, and it howled in the streets, adding to our nervousness. None of us slept that night. I sat up with Lily, but we got the tired child off to sleep in the early morning.

Earthquakes are not very uncommon in Spain and Portugal, and several times I have felt the earth tremble. But this disturbance at Coimbra was really serious, and I must confess that I was greatly alarmed for our safety.

For two or three days the weather continued stormy and wild, and many people feared that there would be another shock. The talk in the hotel and everywhere was about earthquakes and the disaster at Lisbon a few years ago. Some of the inhabitants left the town in a state of alarm.

Our engagement at Coimbra was now at an end. The benefit performance, which had abruptly concluded in such a remarkable manner, only brought us a few pounds after paying the expenses. As for my student friend, he was not to be found, and he had not paid us for the tickets he had sold for our benefit. I was quite mystified. Why had this man, who had professed such an ardent friendship for me, suddenly ceased to come to the performances? Ever since he took the tickets to sell he had carefully avoided meeting me.

I was heartily chaffed by my friends about his disappearance. I did not mind this, but it was exasperating to think that I had been "done" in this manner, and I determined to sift the mystery.

"The fellow deserves imprisonment," said one of the artistes at the café when I told him my tale. "But I do not advise you to make a police case. The law in Portugal is very curious, and if the police do take up the case, you'll have to stay in Coimbra to give evidence."

"I don't wish to inform the police," I said; "but I would like to get the money that he got for the tickets."

At length I decided to go to the college and to look for my cavalier. I attired myself in a quiet black dress and a mantilla, and went up the hill to the university. It was a somewhat strange errand. I don't like dunning people for money; and, besides, this man had represented himself as my friend, and I had liked him. However, the money was not only due to me; it belonged in part to my friends the Gambolis. We were not in a very flourishing way just then. I therefore decided to act immediately.

I felt rather nervous as I came near the imposing building and saw several students emerge. Two of them recognized me, and one raised his hat.

"The English dancer," they murmured.

"Can you tell me where I can find Dom Sebastian?" I asked in Spanish.

"Dom Sebastian?" they repeated. Then one of the students bade me follow him, and he led me to a house in an adjoining street. An old crone answered his summons. As my guide spoke to her she looked me closely up and down and rumpled her yellow forehead. At that moment I saw Dom Sebastian cross the passage of the house. Without ceremony, I pushed by the old woman and went into the house. My prey had entered the parlour, and I knocked at the door.

The features of my friend were a study. He muttered something inaudible, and his cheeks grew pale as I confronted him. His aspect proved that he was guilty.

"I have come for the money that you owe me," I said quietly.

Dom Sebastian drew himself up, and then bowed profoundly.

"I owe you an apology," he stammered. "I have been unfortunate, señorita; I have lost it."

"Lost it?" I repeated, in amazement.

"Let me explain, please?" he said, with another bow. "Be seated, if you please."

I sat down and listened to his story. Never have I seen a man appear so abject as this young Portuguese student. He wrung his hands as if in pain, and his forehead was damp with nervousness. Did he think that I intended to inform the police?

"Señorita," he said in a pathetic tone, "my conduct may seem very base in your eyes. But, believe me, I had no intention of cheating you, and I vow that the money shall be paid to you in full. To tell the whole truth and to hide nothing is my intention. I will tell you, then, that I am in the clutches of moneylenders.

"I have been foolish, señorita; I have gambled heavily, and misfortune has followed me for weeks past. Hoping to pay my debts of honour, I staked the money that I had received for the benefit tickets, and, alas! I lost all."

His voice sank to a sob. I was touched by his emotion, for I still remembered that I had enjoyed his friendship. What could I say? I was sorry for him, but, at the same time, it was unfair that the Gambolis should suffer through his folly.

"Believe me, every reis that I owe you will be paid in a week or two," he declared with his hand at his heart. "Ah, my adorable English lady, I would that I could express to you the admiration that I have for your grace——"

I stopped him in the middle of a fine speech. It seemed to me insincere, and in a flash I divined the man's true character. He was fooling me.

"We are going to-morrow to Evora. I shall call daily at the post office for letters, and I hope you will send the money quickly. Good-day."

"Señorita, one moment," he cried. "I will send you all the money in the course of ten days. I am writing to my mother for money.... I have loved you sincerely——"

"That is enough," I said in a frigid tone.

"Señorita, listen——" he began.

But I went from the room.

CHAPTER VIII

MY PORTUGUESE HOSTS

DID I ever receive the money from him? No, dear reader, I did not. As I walked down the hill from the university I said to myself:

"Put no more trust in that young man. You'll never see that money."

No; Dom Sebastian was a handsome flatterer, that is all. That is the best that can be said for him. I am afraid that he was a born adventurer and a swindler. Well, I had learned a little more of the ways of men, and I intended to profit by the experience.

Perhaps some of my readers will smile at this credulity. They will say that a woman on the stage should have her wits about her. Let me say that I do not like to distrust people; it is not my nature. I have told you enough of my life to show that I had a very hard childhood. I don't think my trials have made me bitter and suspicious of every one that I meet, though they might have had that effect upon me.

And it is a mistake to suppose that because a girl lives a rough-and-tumble life as a performer that she develops cunning, and grows into a designing woman. There are gentle, trusting women " on the boards," as in other walks of life. Of course, I have known girls who were not at all correct in their conduct if they learned that it paid them to cast aside the strict ideas in which they were brought up. But, as I have said before, and wish to repeat, the typist girl is not less tempted to go astray than the average girl on the stage. If a girl wishes to trade upon her good looks, she has opportunities in any occupation that brings her into association with men.

From Coimbra we went to Evora, an old town to the south of Lisbon. It is an astonishment to the artiste in Spain and Portugal to find a town of this size provided with places of entertainment

A DANCING GIRL 149

that are open all the year round and pay the proprietors a good profit. Evora is no bigger than Basingstoke, and not so big as Guildford, yet it had its variety hall.

This delightful town is surrounded by distant mountains, and the scenery is charming. The streets are narrow and quiet, and there are some fine Roman remains of a temple and an aqueduct.

We had a very comfortable engagement at Evora, and I was sorry to leave the place. A rather curious adventure befell us there. Two gentlemen, who lived together in a fine mansion about seven miles from the town, became acquainted with Gamboli. One day they proposed that we should all drive out to their country place and dine with them in the evening. Lily, her little boy, and I rode with one of our hosts in a smart carriage drawn by a fine pair of horses, and Gamboli and the other host rode in another vehicle.

We left Evora at four in the afternoon, and I well remember the beauty of the day as we drove through vineyards and orchards in the bright sunshine. Our hosts were very entertaining and full of high spirits, not to say somewhat boisterous. We left the flat country soon, and the road wound upwards and upwards on a hill-side, with splendid views on every hand.

"There is our house," said the gentleman who rode in our carriage, pointing to a large white building among some tall trees.

It was a most beautiful country house. The grounds were delightfully laid out, and the wild country stretched all around. There were groves of lemon and orange trees and a lovely rose garden, with a fountain and a pond, in which big fish were swimming. Two peacocks strutted in front of the house. From the wood came the loud note of the golden oriole and the cooing of pigeons. It was like a fairy palace.

Within, the house was finely decorated; the walls and ceilings were painted, and the furniture was sumptuous. There were statues in the hall, and fine oil paintings.

Our hosts were both bachelors, and they shared this delightful residence.

There was a small regiment of servants of both sexes to wait upon us. We sat in a veranda overlooking the glowing garden, and the men lit cigars and we all sipped red wine.

After a rest we went to see the horses, and visited the farm, and saw peasants making hay and milking the cows. Everything seemed peaceful and happy, and I envied our hosts' good fortune in possessing such a charming home in this land of sunshine, roses, and wine.

The dinner was of about ten courses, and very well served. Several kinds of wine were on the table, and I noticed that our hosts frequently motioned to the servants to fill our glasses. Champagne flowed like water. Our hosts began to get more hilarious. They cracked jokes, proposed toasts, and made the house ring with their hearty laughter.

Again and again I refused wine. I even kept my hand over my glass when I saw the bottles and decanters coming.

After dinner Mr Gamboli went with one of our hosts, taking little Henry with him, and Lily and I were left with the other host.

By this time both our hosts were exceedingly lively; in fact, the caballero who entertained Lily and myself had taken too much. But he continued to drink and to force liqueurs upon us. Benedictine, Chartreuse, and Crême de Menthe were on the table, and cognac and coffee were brought in.

Our host's manner now became extremely familiar. The wine had emboldened him.

"Enjoy yourselves, ladies! Drink and be happy," he invited us, seizing a bottle and filling our glasses.

I refused repeatedly to drink any more, but our host was persistent. It was his idea of a "spree." Probably there was a sly motive in tempting us in this way. I resolved to keep my head cool.

Where was Mr Gamboli and the boy? Why did they not join us? Our host began to sing uproariously. Presently he leaned across the table to reach a bottle, and in doing so he upset a glass of wine.

"Long live Bacchus!" he cried. "Be merry, ladies, be merry!"

I thought it was time to go in search of Mr Gamboli and little Henry, but Lily begged me not to leave her. Our host was now noisy and reckless beyond all bounds. He flourished his wine-glass, and made even wilder speeches, inviting us to join him in another bottle.

Presently Gamboli and the other host appeared, but the boy was not with them. They had been playing at billiards, and the little fellow was in charge of one of the servants. Lily rose in great concern, for we were in such queer company that we feared that something might have befallen her child.

"Why didn't you keep him with you?" she asked her husband.

"The child is all right," said the host who had just entered.

"Let us be going," whispered Lily to her husband. "It must be very late."

"Don't be in haste," said our host. "Come, let us have a bottle of champagne."

But I for one was anxious to get away, and Lily insisted that she was very tired. So, after a search, little Henry was found in one of the servants' rooms, and the carriage was ordered for our drive back to Coimbra. The livelier of our two hosts was now in a sort of stupor. He sat blinking in his chair, with a half-smoked cigar in the corner of his mouth.

I shall never forget our drive to Coimbra in the dawn. It was just daybreak as we started, and the golden orioles were piping in the woods. In the distance the mountains shone rosy in the light of the rising sun, and soon the sky was barred and striped with orange and mauve. The air was sweet and fresh, and I breathed it with relief after the hours we had spent in the fumes of wine and cigars. Little Henry dozed, with his head on his mother's shoulder, and Gamboli was drowsy. But I was wide awake, and I was sorry when we came in sight of the town, for I had never enjoyed the beauties of a summer sunrise so much.

We were now nearing the end of our tour in Spain and Portugal. Our next town was Vigo, one of the chief ports of northern Spain.

From Vigo we went to Santander, and on to the busy town of Bilbao. Here the outlook seemed rather dismal, for although there is a theatre and a circus in the town, there were not, at that time, any singing cafés. It was the first town we had visited in Spain where there was no building in which we could perform.

When things were looking rather serious Gamboli, who was never daunted by difficulties, persuaded the proprietor of a café to erect a little stage, and to introduce a variety show to his patrons. We went on sharing terms, and the scheme turned out a fair success; but we could not make money out of the venture. So at the request of a café proprietor in San Sebastian, we moved on to that town after spending about three months at Bilbao.

San Sebastian was the last town in Spain in which I danced. I often wished afterwards that I had stayed with my good friends, the Gambolis, and gone with them to Switzerland and Italy. But I had been away from England for three years, and I began to yearn for a sight of the old country. More than all, I wanted to see some one to whom I was strongly attached. The temptation was too powerful to be resisted. I was within about sixty hours' journey of London, and I had saved a little money out of my Spanish tour. So, for good or ill, I determined to return to England.

I was deeply moved when the time came for me to say "Good-bye" to my friends and to leave beautiful, sunny Spain, where I had passed so many happy days.

I was glad when I reached London. But, oh, the greyness of the sky, the dinginess of the streets, and the racket and roar! I thought I should never get used to London life again. And very soon I began to realize how much keener the fight for a living is in this country than in Spain or France. At least, it is so for those who call themselves artistes, and who live by amusing the public. I am not clever enough to explain why this is so, for England is such a rich country, and there is no scarcity of variety halls or theatres.

CHAPTER IX

HARD TIMES IN LONDON

WELL, I was back in London, and I realized that I was at home. I was perhaps a little disappointed with England. I had hardly a relative living, and my few friends were scattered.

For three years I had been fortunate. Rarely had I been out of an engagement for longer than a week. But now my luck turned. My small savings began to melt. Remember that I had kept myself by hook and by crook from the age of twelve, and always kept my contracts, and tried my best to please the public. And yet I came back to England to find want staring me in the face.

I had now reached a rather tragic

period of my career. I was almost in despair, and matters did not mend till a chance turned up to appear as a solo dancer in a pantomime. There were still weeks to wait before I could handle any of my salary; but the prospect of an engagement filled me with new hope and encouragement.

The pantomime in which I was engaged was "The House that Jack Built." I hoped that great things would come of this contract. A solo dancer has the stage to herself, if only for a few minutes; and she is more "in the picture" than when performing with a troupe. In Spain and France I had often danced by myself. I was considered clever enough for Paris, Madrid, Barcelona, Oporto, and other big Continental towns. "Surely," I thought, "I ought to make a hit in a suburban theatre in England."

During the weeks before the production of the annual pantomimes there is much excitement and anxiety among the artistes. The "stars" are, of course, booked for many months, and often years, ahead. But the less fortunate performers suffer agonies of misgiving and uncertainty concerning their chances of a good engagement in the pantomime. And, after all, with the best of good fortune, the minor actor or actress can only reckon on a run of eight or twelve weeks. A "star" will make anything from £100 to £300 a week during the pantomime season, and often earn more in one week than many artistes can earn in a year.

Many of the variety performers owe their success to popularity in pantomime. A good song will often make an artiste's fortune. Dancers, unless they possess pleasant singing voices, stand a small chance of winning their way to favour in pantomime; and even a good voice counts for little if the song is not what the audience wants.

Just before the pantomimes the lucky artistes who are "booked" are in high spirits. It is astonishing how hopeful we are in the profession, in spite of bad times. On the whole, we complain very little about our trials, and the public at large think we have an easy time. Six months' experience of an artiste's life would teach many people a severe lesson. The public see only the brightly-lighted side of the picture; there is another side, and it is often gloomy enough. But of that side only the artistes know.

We were soon rehearsing " The House that Jack Built." As I had no lines in the pantomime, I was not required until it was time to go on the stage and give my dance. But I attended rehearsals punctually.

A pantomime rehearsal is a rather drab affair. Most theatres look dingy in the daytime, and on a raw December day a number of actors and actresses, in their everyday garb, cutting capers, and muttering their dialogue, do not look particularly interesting or amusing. The principal boy will look majestic on Boxing Night, clad in her tights and jewels, but during the rehearsal she seems a very ordinary sort of young woman.

As for the comedians, they are often disappointing during the rehearsals. The manager and the stage-manager put their heads together and whisper: " When is he going to be funny? The show seems fearfully dull." But the comedian, whether he plays the baron or the dame, will be a different man on the opening night. He does not feel the part until he is dressed for it, and he wants the audience before him to put him on his mettle.

The public have only a slight idea of the work and anxiety involved in the production of a Christmas pantomime. For months the scene-painters are at work, and extra hands are engaged in making the scenery and accessories. The making of the costumes occupies a small company of seamstresses, and in some theatres all the dresses are designed and made on the premises.

This was my first pantomime engagement, and I took a special interest in everything connected with it. I made friends among the girls in the dressing-rooms, and found plenty of kindness. But it seemed very fresh and strange to me, as I had been abroad for so long and had lived with foreigners. Yet artistes are alike in certain ways all the world over.

They are used to ups and downs, and this induces a feeling of comradeship.

"The House that Jack Built" was a success. The pantomime went with a swing, and every one in the company worked hard. After the London run, the pantomime was booked for the Crewe Theatre and other provincial towns. But a terrible disaster befell us at Crewe.

We started for Crewe in good spirits, taking with us all the scenery and properties of "The House that Jack Built."

I was glad to have a peep once more at the fresh green country, for London seemed a grey and rather dismal place after my long absence among the beautiful old Moorish towns of Spain, where fogs are unknown and a dull sky is seldom seen. I was happy and contented, for there was a chance of the pantomime running for a few more weeks.

No one can understand fate and luck. Why was I in luck for three years with hardly a break? And why was I now doomed to a spell of hard misfortune? These things are beyond our control, and they have nothing to do with one's ability.

The pantomime went very well at Crewe at the first performance. I felt well and cheerful, and forgot the hardships of the past months. Then came a swift and awful calamity.

One night after the show my friend and I dawdled over our dressing while we chatted. I am always rather slow in changing my costume, and I think we were amongst the last of the artistes to leave the theatre. We walked to our lodgings, ate some supper, and went to bed, feeling tired after the performance.

Just as I began to doze I was conscious of some one calling in the street. I turned over, and took no notice. But the shouting continued, and I sat up and listened.

"Girls, girls, get up—fire!" was the cry that reached my sleepy brain.

I could not believe my ears. However, I aroused my friend, who was fast asleep.

And going to the window, and pulling the blind aside, I saw in the street two men of the pantomime company waving their arms.

"The theatre is on fire!" they shouted loudly.

"Never!" cried my companion, who came to the window, rubbing her eyes.

"It is true," I said in great consternation, for I saw a fiery glare in the sky, and heard shouts of alarm in the streets.

"Oh, we shall lose all our things," said my friend.

"Let us run to the theatre as fast as we can," said I, beginning to dress in frantic haste.

In a few minutes we were dressed, and, putting on our hats, we rushed down the stairs and into the street. Men were running towards the theatre. A fire-engine dashed along. We followed it, running as quickly as we could.

I shall never forget the fearful spectacle of that blazing theatre. About an hour ago we had been in the building. Now the flames were raging everywhere, and darting fierce tongues through the windows. The whole town was lit up in the glare.

We shuddered at the thought that some of the theatre staff might still be in the theatre. But fortunately every one had escaped. The engines were soon at work, and the firemen directed the hose on to the neighbouring buildings, which were in danger.

"We shall lose all our costumes and things," moaned my friend.

"They are ashes by now," I said.

"And it's the end of the pantomime, too," said a member of the company who had joined us.

I watched the fire with a hopeless sinking in my heart. Yes, it was the end of my short run of good luck. Bit by bit the theatre was being devoured, and the firemen, though they worked desperately, utterly failed to subdue the fierce flames. Myriads of sparks went dancing up into the blackness of the night, and a dense cloud of smoke floated above the town.

Tears came into my eyes. My companions were silent. We all realized that nothing could have been done to save the scenery, properties, and costumes, for the fire had spread with amazing rapidity throughout the entire building. All the beautiful dresses were now ashes. For myself, I possessed hardly anything but the clothes I stood in.

For an hour we waited in the cold, raw air, gazing at the burning theatre. Then we went our ways, all of us made dumb by the catastrophe. My friend and I could not sleep that morning. We saw the dawn break, and with the coming of daylight we seemed to realize more acutely the difficulty of our position.

"What's to be done?" I said feebly. "The show can't go on; everything is destroyed."

"I don't know," murmured my friend. "It is just awful; too awful for words!"

"Well," I said, "I've been in an earthquake, I've nearly been shipwrecked, I've almost been smashed to pieces in a fall from the flying rings, and now I've just escaped being burned to death. I wonder what's coming next. It's a pretty good record for a woman of twenty-two."

"What about our salaries?" asked my friend.

"Yes, what indeed?" I muttered as we turned away from the blackened ruins of the theatre.

Could any outlook seem worse? We were stranded, or, in other words, "on the rocks." Our manager was a heavy loser, and we were all sufferers together, from the principals down to the humblest member of the company. For some of the girls the situation was terrible, for they had been out of engagements for some time, and were hoping to recover their losses and pay their debts. We could only console one another by repeating:

"Well, we're all in the same boat."

We knew, of course, that this was the end of the provincial tour of "The House that Jack Built." Not a trace of that pantomime survived. And it was too late in the season to start afresh. We were all suddenly thrown out of employment in the worst time of the year. There was no chance of any more pantomime engagements.

Some of us had not the price of our fares back to London. It was a miserable predicament, and we wondered how we were going to wriggle out of it.

The public are, as a rule, kind to artistes. A number of the influential people of Crewe were very sympathetic, and they came to the rescue of the unfortunate company of "The House that Jack Built." To relieve our distress, a benefit performance was to be given at the Town Hall. The town was billed, and we hoped that the proceeds of the entertainment would repay us for the dresses that we had lost in the fire.

Our company was a large one, and though the Town Hall was fairly filled, there was not much to divide amongst us.

I came back to London with several members of the company. I went into lodgings with some friends, and began to look up advertisements and to call regularly on my agent. Every effort that

I made to obtain work was fruitless. No troupe of dancers were needed at this time of the year. The pantomime season was drawing to an end, and there seemed to be no vacancies on the halls.

Day after day I tramped about the theatrical quarter, meeting artistes who, like myself, were "waiting for dates." The army of the unemployed acrobats, dancers, and actors increased when the pantomimes came to an end. Everywhere I met acquaintances down on their luck. Heaven knows how some of us live in the long periods of "resting." Yet if an artiste is shabby and down-at-heel his fate is written plainly; he will receive coldness wherever he calls.

I have found London a terribly cruel place for a young girl. But I will not exaggerate, for I have met with kindness in unexpected quarters. Certainly, the wage-earning class are exceedingly brotherly towards one another.

I found that during my absence from England I had lost touch of the acrobatic folk, and my efforts to trace friends were unsuccessful. How was I to live? This question gnawed at my brain every hour of the day and often by night.

I have reached the most painful stage in my journey since the day when I ran away. How much I had learned since that time nearly eleven years ago. At all events, during my apprenticeship I always had food enough, but now I could see nothing before me but want.

How could I turn my hand to some other employment than the stage? I had never experienced what is known as home life. Most of the eleven years had been spent in lodgings and in hotels, and in travelling from town to town. I stood no chance of competing for a business post, for I knew nothing of business.

A little gleam of hope came when a man, of whom I had never heard, applied to the dancing school for an artiste who could dance in the Spanish style. I was to call upon this man, who would give me particulars.

I arrived early at his office. He had not arrived. When he came in he asked me if I knew the bolero, the jota, and the

A DANCING GIRL

Sevilliana. I replied that I knew the first two dances very well, but not the last.

"You look Spanish," he said.

"I am not Spanish, but I have lived for three years in Spain, and danced at Madrid, Barcelona, San Sebastian, and other towns," was my reply.

"Well, that accounts for the way you wear your hair," he said. "You certainly have a Spanish appearance. Now, I want you to see an Italian gentleman, a leader of an orchestra, who requires a dancer in the Spanish style. He lives here." And he wrote down the address on a piece of paper, and handed it to me.

The Italian leader of the orchestra lived in Bayswater, and I went to his house, carrying my dancing costume and some music. He was a polite, vivacious gentleman, and he began to tell me of a scheme for introducing a *café chantant* entertainment in London.

"I require a dancer, one who can dance in the Spanish style, play the castanets, and sing a few songs. The salary will be two pounds ten a week, and the hours seven to eleven each night."

As I was anxious to get work, I gladly accepted the terms offered.

"Now, I have tried to find a good dancer, but I have failed. The English girls are able to dance, but it is dancing without feeling, without passion.

"I want a lively dancer," he continued, "and she must sing to the violin, mandoline, and guitar. Will you let me see you dance?"

"Certainly," I said. "Will you have a Spanish dance?"

"Yes, that will do," returned the conductor, taking up my music and sitting down at the piano.

Well, I performed several dances. My heart jumped when he praised my performance of the bolero. Was my bad luck going to turn? I danced in several styles, and he watched me critically while he played the accompaniment. Then he tried my voice in one or two songs. But he did not like my songs. He seemed difficult to please, and I began to surmise that nothing would come of the interview.

My guess was correct. Luck was against me, and I went away terribly disappointed.

At the Marble Arch I turned into the park, and wandered, hardly knowing where I went. I was tired, hungry, and sad, and bitter thoughts rose in my brain as I watched the well-dressed, over-fed daughters of the fashionable world driving by. It seemed to me that they surveyed their poorer brothers and sisters with scorn.

I felt unwanted in the world as I sank to a seat in the Row. My life had proved a strange one since I entered the variety profession, and just now I could only dwell on the darker side of it. I yearned for a friend, an adviser, a sympathizer. Here in England I was more lonely than I had ever felt in Spain or France.

After sitting for some time in the park I made my way to the Surrey side, pursued by gloomy anticipations, and much depressed by the result of my interview with the Italian musician. I had promised that I would let the gentleman who had given me the introduction hear the result of my interview. Accordingly I called upon him on the following day.

Mr —— was a sympathetic man, and he told me afterwards that he knew directly I returned to the room that I had not been successful.

"You're on the rocks, aren't you?"

"Yes," I answered; "I have had a long run of bad luck."

He thought for a moment, and then said:

"I may still be able to help you. Take this as an advance on any engagement that I may obtain for you."

And he put some money into my hand. I did not like to accept this loan, and I told him that I was in debt. He encouraged me to talk, and it was a relief to me to speak of my difficulties and disappointments. He listened very attentively.

"I am an author," he said, and he pointed to a row of books that he had written. "Why don't you write your life? It would interest many people, as it has interested me."

The idea of writing a book had never entered my head.

"I'm afraid I couldn't write my life," I said humbly.

"Yes you could if you tried," he returned in a most encouraging tone. "You have all the material for an entertaining history of stage life. We have had plenty of biographies of people on the stage who have reached the top of the ladder, but there would be freshness and novelty in a story of your career from the time that you ran away from home. Now try to write the story, naturally and simply, as you have told it to me, and I think I can get it published for you."

He gave me a few suggestions about this story, and then he asked me to have lunch with him. I was greatly cheered. I felt that things were not quite hopeless after all.

In the meantime I happened to meet an old friend in the acrobatic profession, who told me that he was finding artistes for a series of gala performances in Wales.

The open-air gala was to be held at Swansea, in South Wales, in the centre of an iron and coal district. The organizers hoped that the performances would draw for several days, and I was cheered that the engagement might last for two or three weeks, for it was suggested that galas should be given in other manufacturing centres of South Wales.

I arranged to give a horizontal-bar turn, which was to last eight minutes. The performances were to be given twice a day, in the afternoon and the evening. Almost all the turns were of a sensational acrobatic character. I was acquainted with two or three of the artistes engaged, and I agreed to travel down with them on the Saturday preceding Bank Holiday.

But although this chance had come in my way as a pleasant surprise, I was now faced by a serious difficulty. The third-class fare to Swansea is sixteen shillings and sixpence-halfpenny. I was able to borrow nine shillings from the friends with whom I lived, but this was all that

I could get. On the Friday morning I had only raised nine shillings.

I was nearly desperate when I sat down and wrote to Mr ——, the author whom I have mentioned, asking him if he would lend me enough money to make up my fare, and promising to repay him on my return from South Wales.

The letter reached its destination about five o'clock in the afternoon. At six o'clock I received this telegram: "Certainly. Meet me Trafalgar Square at 7.30." My heart gave a great bound of surprise and joy.

CHAPTER X

WITH A TROUPE IN AMERICA

YOU may be sure that I was at Trafalgar Square punctually at half-past seven. My friend—for so I regarded him now—was waiting for me near the Nelson Column. He shook my hand, cutting me short when I began to thank him. He proposed that we should go into St James's Park, and sit down under the trees. It was a lovely, warm evening after a showery day, and the park looked fresh and green.

"Look here," said my friend, "We are both artistes, aren't we? We live by amusing the public, you as a dancer, and I as a writer. We have both known bitter hardships and trials, and this has made us both sympathetic. Now, if I were in your position and came to you for temporary assistance, would you refuse me?"

"Oh, of course not," I said.

"Very well, then, there is no merit in my offering you a small sum of money; so don't feel that you are under a great obligation to me."

I think my voice trembled a little as I thanked him."

"Now, tell me all about the gala," he said.

I told him I thought something might come of this engagement, and I described the terms on which I was working. He seemed troubled that I should have to return to the acrobatic business after my success as a dancer in France, Switzerland, and Spain.

"You'll have to make a name as a speciality dancer," he said. "I'm sure it's in you if you only got the chance."

I went back to my lodgings feeling much happier. A great weight of care had been lifted from my mind, and I slept calmly that night.

The next morning I started hopefully for Swansea with some of the artistes. After the long journey we had to search for lodgings, a dreary business at the best of times. That day I walked about for three hours before I could find a room to let within my means. At last, in a back street, I found a woman who would take me in; and tired and hungry, I ate a meal and went to bed.

The ground where the gala was to be held was outside the town, in a field. A dressing tent is provided on these occasions for the performers, but the accommodation is rough, and often the tent is cold and draughty. The weather had been wet for days, and the ground was soaked and muddy. It was a cheerless summer, and Bank Holiday in August proved a rainy day.

In an enclosure the gymnastic apparatus had been erected—the bars, rings, and the slack wire for a wire-walking turn. I tested my bar and found it all right.

As I had not practised gymnastics for a long time, my hands were soft, and they were quickly blistered. On the third day I had a bad blister on the left hand, which gave me some pain.

We were all surprised and disappointed when we learned that our services would not be required after the third day. Some of us had come from London, and our railway fares and lodging expenses had eaten up all our salaries. It was not worth coming for. The wire-walking artiste was terribly disappointed, and so, indeed, were all of us in the company. Instead of having a few shillings over, I was out of pocket.

I returned to London with a cold, caught through performing in the rain, blistered hands, and an empty purse.

Circumstances now compelled me to leave my lodgings and find a bed-sitting room at a few shillings a week.

For forty-eight hours I had nothing to eat or drink except a slice of bread-and-butter and a cup of tea.

I have more than once found truth in the saying that the darkest hour is just before the dawn. In my last chapter I have told how near I was to starvation, and how utterly hopeless I felt. I was in my lowest depths when a note came from my literary friend. He asked how I was getting on, and said that he was still trying to find an engagement for me.

The letter comforted me. There was at least *one* person in London who was thinking about me, and I felt that I could tell him everything. So I wrote at once to say how I was situated. It is very hard to bear one's troubles in silence and quite alone.

Half an hour after receiving my letter Mr —— was at the corner of the road. He sent a messenger to me with this brief note: " Meet me in ten minutes at the corner of the street." That very morning I had been asked to go to the dancing school, and help with a class of pupils; and when my friend's note came I was putting on my hat. With my practice dress in brown paper, I hurried down the stairs and went to the meeting-place.

Mr —— was very concerned. He took my hand, and there was a painful expression on his face when he said:

"Good heavens, this will never do! It's too dreadful to think about. I came at once. Look here, you must get some food this minute."

"I can't," I replied. "I have to be at the school in half an hour. How good of you to come. How can I thank you?"

"Don't try to thank me," he said. "It makes me angry, quite furious, to think that anyone should be in such a plight. You must get food, I say, and at once."

"I don't feel that I need it," I returned. "I can wait for a few hours. I've got beyond wanting food."

"I won't have it," he said firmly. "I'm going to be very strict with you because you want looking after, and I don't want to lose a good artiste."

I am quite sure that truth is stranger than the strangest fiction that was ever written. In stories and plays when a woman is in distress a rescuer arrives at the nick of time and saves her. This is a tale of actual life. Quite by accident I made the acquaintance of this man, who proved my friend in need. What might have happened if we had never met? I could not think. It was my very darkest hour. The incident seems to me even now a miracle as I look back upon it, and Mr —— is like an imaginary character.

And now my luck began to turn. Two offers of engagements reached me within the next few days. One was from a musical comedy company that was going on tour. Two dancers were required by the management. The other opening was in a troupe of girl dancers, to perform for three months, and probably longer, in Buenos Ayres, in the Argentine. I was very delighted with these offers. I wrote to my friend, telling him of my good luck, and seeking his advice. He advised me to give a trial show for the musical comedy company.

"It is well to make sure of both chances," he said.

I arranged, therefore, to dance before the management at eleven o'clock on the appointed morning. With the usual nervousness experienced by artistes who have to give a trial, I went to the place, and found a number of girls assembled. It was an anxious-looking crowd. My partner in the dance was the shorter of the pair, and I was told that both of the girls must be of the same height. We danced as directed, and no fault was found with my performance. But I was too tall. So, with regret, the manager dismissed me.

"Well, it will have to be South America," I said to myself, as I gained the street.

I called on my friend, and told him what had happened.

"Very well, it's fate," he said. "South

America is a long way off, and if the contract only lasts for three months it seems hardly worth going."

"But it's work," I said, "and I long to be in employment again. I love foreign countries, and I'd like to see the Argentine."

I closed at once with the agent's offer, and then began one of the busiest weeks that I have ever spent. We were well-trained performers, but we had to learn a set of special new dances for this engagement. To do this in the limited time at our disposal meant hard work daily, from ten in the morning till seven in the evening, with a short interval for lunch and tea.

Imagine us, then, eight girls—all young and, if I may say so, good-looking—dressed in our practising clothes, going through, hour after hour, the intricate steps of an eccentric dance, a graceful dance, a skipping-rope dance, a step dance, and four others. Special songs had to be learned as well. And this was not all, for we had to have our new costumes made. In the few spare hours left I covered several pairs of ballet shoes with pink satin.

I was appointed the interpreter for the troupe, for I knew Spanish; and it was my business to see that the girls kept up their practice on board ship. The members of the troupe looked to me for help in various ways.

We had our photographs taken by a theatrical photographer for advertising purposes, and in one of them we looked rather quaint in sunbonnets and children's frocks. Then there was shopping to do, dress-baskets to pack, and a hundred and one things that occupied every minute of the day.

The management paid our second-class fares to and from Buenos Ayres to London. Then we steamed slowly down the Mersey, and I bade farewell to England.

I am used to travelling by sea, and I am usually what is called "a good sailor." But never shall I forget the horrors of the Bay of Biscay. It was a terribly stormy passage from Liverpool to Vigo, and when we reached the dangerous

Bay the storm raged furiously. I was too ill to leave my berth for two days.

At last we reached Vigo, the lovely town where I had spent many happy days with the two Gambolis. As the ship stayed there for a few hours I went ashore, and was glad to think that I was in Spain once more. Vigo seemed as sunny and lovely as ever.

The life on a great liner is delightful in fine weather. We sat in the sunshine on deck chairs, enjoying the breeze and pleasant motion of the vessel, eating bananas and melons, and laughing and joking. The sea air did me an immense amount of good. I regained my spirits, slept comfortably, and found life more tolerable than it had been for months past. However, a mishap befell me at Lisbon, which caused me much anxiety.

A gentleman on board, who had been friendly to me, asked me to go ashore and see the sights of the city. We went to the cathedral, and climbed a hill for a view of the place, and in walking I blistered my left heel through wearing an uncomfortable shoe. I took no notice of the blister, but in a few days blood-poisoning set in, and I was quite lame.

This was a source of great worry to me. What would happen if I was unable to dance in Beunos Ayres? How unfortunate that a few hours on shore should have caused this serious trouble. The doctor was very attentive and kind, and he told me not to get anxious; but I could not help feeling alarmed at my lameness. The injury to my heel prevented me from practising my dances in the early morning on deck with the other girls. It also interfered with pleasure, for I was not able to join in the dances at a ball that was given in the saloon. I sat watching the dances, feeling rather gloomy.

But, fortunately, my foot healed in a week or two, and when we reached the Rio Plata I was better, and able to dance again.

The voyage to Buenos Ayres occupied three weeks, but the time seemed to pass quickly. At each port I posted a letter to my author-friend, telling him about my doings on board, and at the various

A DANCING GIRL

places where we had been ashore for a few hours.

At last we reached Buenos Ayres. It was a Sunday in September, and people were going about the busy streets wrapped in furs and cloaks, for it was still the cold season.

In the evening we all went to the theatre. We were not impressed by the look of the outside of the building, which seemed dreary. Some repairs were being done to the front of the house, and the scaffolding was not ornamental. Upon giving our names we were received by the manager, who welcomed us to the Argentine, and asked us if we would like to see the performance. We expressed a wish to see the show, so we were given seats.

The Theatre Royal of Buenos Ayres is the principal place of amusement in the city. It is a sort of variety palace. Instead of the ordinary music-hall " numbers," a *revue* is written, and all the artistes take part in it, giving their turns as they do in pantomime in England. The *revue* that night was in French. It seemed to me an attractive show. We were all very keen when a troupe of English dancers came on the stage. Could they " give us points," or were we better than them?

Well, I don't wish to boast; but we watched the troupe very critically, and came to the conclusion that we need not fear following them.

The cost of living in Buenos Ayres was higher than I had expected, and the hotel charges were a great drain on our salaries. In fact, Buenos Ayres cannot be called a cheap place to live in, and although we earned more than we should have earned in London it was difficult to leave any margin over.

Before coming to South America we had heard some queer stories about the fast life of Buenos Ayres. On the stage one is supposed to be more able to form an opinion on this subject than in other occupations. It was soon plain to me that if an artiste wants to live what is called " a gay life " she has plenty of opportunities in this city. There are wealthy and dissolute persons here, as in every other big city that I have visited. But whether Buenos Ayres is worse in this respect than London, Paris, or Berlin, I am not able to say.

I have now reached the end of my true story of life on the variety stage. For nearly twelve years I have experienced all the ups and downs of the performer's life, and most of that period has been spent on the Continent, moving frequently from place to place. It is one of the drawbacks of the profession that we know very little of the quiet, settled feeling of those who have fixed places of residence. For years I have hardly realized the meaning of the word " home," for my occupation has kept me continually on the move.

But what I may have lost in one way I have gained in another. I have seen many lands, and met many kinds of people at home and abroad. I have lived under the shadow of the magnificent Alps; I have strolled in the sunlit streets of the ancient Moorish cities of Spain; I have seen the life of Paris and Brussels, and other great towns of the Continent. I suppose there are not a great many girls of my age who have had such experiences. The reader may perhaps be curious to know whether I would change my profession for any other. I do not wish to leave the stage. It is my ambition to excel in my art, which is one of the oldest in the world. And I should like to act in drama. I am still young, although I have seen so much, and there stretches before me the future, vague, but full of chances and possibilities.

One thing I think I have learned from my various experiences, and that is a sort of understanding of men and women that makes one hesitate before condemning the greatest sinner.

THE END

www.ingramcontent.com/pod-product-compliance
Lightning Source LLC
LaVergne TN
LVHW061214060426
835507LV00016B/1921